"Thank you for the opportunity to meet Leslie; little Leslie, Big Leslie, Candy, and the Leslie who has made the journey to find herself. The Leslie that God always loved and who wept with her through the running and the darkness to become the Leslie that she was meant to be. . . . This book is not about the darkness, but about the way Leslie found the light and the grace-filled God who walked with her every step of the way."

—Jo Lembo, Director of Faith Initiatives and National
Outreach at Shared Hope International

"Leslie King's harrowing experience as a young woman surviving on the streets while facing sexual exploitation, substance use disorder, and shocking violence, is tragically not rare. But her transformation from victim to champion truly inspires. She has returned to those same shadowy corners to help others fight their way out and has committed her life to saving theirs. She offers love and hope to all who are suffering and instructs others who have the power to help. A must-read for all medical professionals."

Leslie Pelkey, MD, FACP, Leslie King's long-standing
primary care physician

"The in-depth world of sex trafficking is dark and filled with things you think only happen on television. Leslie helps you to understand that sex trafficking can hit close to home and any family can be impacted by it. Our community is blessed to have her using her testimony for the greater good."

—Senita Lenear, Third Ward Commissioner,
City of Grand Rapids, Michigan

"This book is a powerful read! Leslie takes you on a journey into her life. Each chapter has you hanging on, anticipating the ending. Everyone needs to own a copy of the book."
—Tashawna "Political Princess" Gill, Political Advisor to Michigan's Governor Gretchen Whitmer

"Leslie is a fierce advocate for women. I am amazed and in awe of her story. She tells a story that needs to be heard and shared with the world. This is a 'must-read' for everyone. It is honest and based on facts. I salute Leslie and her work."
—Tyrone Carter, Michigan State Representative, District 6

"*When Angels Fight* is a brave memoir of God's passionate love to save his children. Leslie King shares her vulnerable story of redemption and, in so doing, teaches all of us how to love and minister to those we often judge and dismiss. Christians are called by Jesus to love the downtrodden; I am grateful Leslie has stepped up to be our guide."
—Noah Filipiak, founding pastor of Mosaic Church in Grand Rapids, Michigan, and author of *Beyond the Battle: A Man's Guide to His Identity in Christ in an Oversexualized World*

WHEN ANGELS FIGHT

WHEN ANGELS FIGHT

My Story of Escaping
Sex Trafficking and Leading a
Revolt Against the Darkness

Leslie F. King

KREGEL
PUBLICATIONS

When Angels Fight: My Story of Escaping Sex Trafficking and Leading a Revolt Against the Darkness
© 2022 by Leslie F. King

Published by Kregel Publications, a division of Kregel Inc., 2450 Oak Industrial Dr. NE, Grand Rapids, MI 49505.

Cataloging-in-Publication Data is available from the Library of Congress.

ISBN 978-0-8254-4689-4, print
ISBN 978-0-8254-7734-8, epub
ISBN 978-0-8254-6839-1, Kindle

Printed in the United States of America
22 23 24 25 26 27 28 29 / 5 4 3 2 1

To my family

CONTENTS

Foreword by Rebecca Bender. 11
Introduction. 15

1. What's Love? 17
2. The Process. 31
3. The Stroll 44
4. Staying. 57
5. Hitting the Bottom 70
6. Freedom 84
7. Life Renewed. 98
8. Moving Forward 115
9. Rebirth. 128
10. Life Lessons. 145

Conclusion. 160
Acknowledgments. 163
Suggested Resources 165
About the Author 169

FOREWORD

eslie King is a modern-day Hosea, inviting us into a world many have never seen and showing us the relentless pursuit of God. Poured out onto each page is her heart and soul, in order to open your eyes and put tangible stories and context to the issues of human trafficking and sexual exploitation. But this book is more than that. These pages are steeped with passion that will inspire you, equip you, and empower you to go help the lost and vulnerable in your very own community.

When you hear the words *sex trafficking*, what comes to mind? Generally, certain images, scenes, and scenarios play out as a moving picture in our minds. But these two simple yet complex words carry a myriad of layers and nuances. Leslie pulls the curtain back on that stereotypical picture and walks us onto the streets, revealing how prostitution in America operates and thrives. The demand for sex, the vulnerabilities of young girls modeling what they were shown in childhood, desensitization to abuse, the innate human need to love and be loved, and the vicious cycle we find ourselves spiraling in—that is the true picture of trafficking.

When you fully understand these complexities, sex trafficking will play a different scene in your mind: a scene like Leslie's and like mine and like the many women who have been trapped in this dangerous underground world. It will break stereotypes of kidnapped, blonde-haired toddlers and open your heart to compassion for the women who are caught in cycles of prostitution, childhood abuse, and trafficking—intersectionalities that are rarely isolated experiences.

Decades ago, our country changed the way Americans saw smoking. Prior to the campaign against this community health risk, one could witness a doctor lighting up in a hospital room or a flight attendant offering Marlboros on an airplane with a smile. It took years and dozens of people standing up to do their parts. It took lawyers who thought outside the box and sued the tobacco industry for health expenses incurred by cancer patients who smoked. It took whistleblowers like Jeffrey Wigand who risked everything—death threats, joblessness, divorce, and lack of money—all to come forward in hopes of making a difference. It took advocates and the media joining together to sound the alarm.

As a teenager, I vividly remember watching anti-smoking commercials on MTV. Hundreds of people spread out on the streets and sidewalks in front of big-tobacco headquarters, representing the number of people who had died of lung cancer. As I got older, I learned of the policymakers and lobbyists who fought to ensure that the public was made more aware of the health risks of smoking that had long been hidden. I learned about all the research on addiction, nicotine, and cancer. Because of all of these moving pieces over time, if you are old enough to remember, you had a front-row seat for watching American culture shift. Smoking is no longer the "safe" habit it was once thought to be, with warnings about the dangers of smoking front and center.

Similarly, the anti-trafficking movement has been around for many years. We have been honored to watch incredible progress in so many areas, and yet there is still an enormous amount of work to be done. It will take all of us coming together and playing our parts to shift the tacit acceptance of sexual exploitation: researchers, advocates, activists, campaigners, concerned citizens, professionals dedicating their skill sets, and those with inside information braving great risk to sound the alarm.

Leslie is one of those women who stood up when it was not popular, who risked it all to come forward. Like many survivors, she has been through hardship that most people will never understand. Her stepping out to share that truth is an immense sacrifice. She also has the strength and resiliency to lean in and push through for the greater good of change, knowing firsthand that redemption and greatness are possible.

With unwavering strength and vulnerability, Leslie puts all her cards on the table to help each of us become better activists, advocates, and change makers. To shift a nation, it will take all of us, and Leslie is a leader who will help take us there.

REBECCA BENDER
Survivor leader, author, speaker,
and CEO and founder of Elevate Academy

INTRODUCTION

I was a runner. Not the one-hundred-yard-dash kind of runner, but the run-away-from-home kind. I ran away from the violence in my childhood home. I ran away from sexual abuse at the hands of a cousin. I ran away from school and juvenile detention. As I began to heal from years of trauma, I realized that I really ran away from fear, loneliness, and defeat.

I didn't know where I was running to, just that I needed to run. It was like I wanted to get out of my skin, to get out of me, and I thought running would help. But everyplace I ran, I was still there. I felt like I was going to explode. I had all these emotions I didn't know what to do with, and that threatened to wreck me. Feelings of anger, feelings about not fitting in with other children. And I was holding in a secret that was literally tearing me apart. I was afraid of everything and angry because of what was happening to me.

I would watch *The Brady Bunch* and *The Partridge Family* on television and imagine that their families were how all families should be. But my family was nothing like those TV families. I went to church and heard that God made us and loves us and takes care of the little children. I didn't feel taken care of at all, wondering how the God I heard about in church could allow all this pain. The only love I saw was violent, with lots of blood, screaming, and begging to please stop.

When my mother had to go to work and my father didn't come home to care for us, my mother took us around the corner to a day care. I remember sitting in that day care bathroom with my hands over my ears because I could still hear her screams from the beating the night before. I wanted my mother's desperate voice to go away, but it never did. The visuals and shrieks never stopped. So I ran.

Little did I know I ran right into the darkness, into the arms of the man whom I thought would love me—only to sell me for years. Who fathered one of my sons, and who put me in charge of other young women he lured and trapped into a life of prostitution.

I ran like the terrified child I was and didn't stop running for over twenty years.

Now, in my midfifties, I can look back and see how God took me out of that life and into one that involves helping women who have similar pasts, who experience mental and physical health issues, and who feel barrelfuls of guilt for events that were beyond their control. I can help others stop their running because God helped me stop mine.

Make no mistake, God and his angels are out there fighting. Will you join them in the revolt against the darkness?

Chapter 1

WHAT'S LOVE?

I was only five. I remember the dull thwacks and sharp cracks of my dad's fists and palms connecting with my mom's body.

"Where the f--- you been?" as he hit her arms. "Where's my food?" as he shoved her into the counter.

Sometimes the hits came without words. Those times were the worst, when the hitting went on and on and my mom's whimpering turned into screaming and pleading. She went to work bruised and bloody many times.

We heard a lot, despite my brother and sister and I crouching in the closet or taking off outside if the weather was decent. My dad was a drinker, an angry alcoholic, and took out his anger on my mom two or three times every week. Often he beat her senseless in his drunken rages, not caring that his children were watching and listening.

"Please stop, please stop, please stop," we heard my mom scream.

When peace returned to the house, we heard my dad say "I love you" to my mom. He seemed to enjoy her company when he wasn't drinking. It didn't last, though; it never did. It wasn't long before he'd disappear to a friend's house or the front porch or the neighborhood bar to start the ugly process all over again. He didn't work, claiming disability after getting hurt on the job. He used crutches to help him walk, and I never saw him without those crutches. Perhaps this contributed to the drinking, or perhaps not. Maybe he was just a mean drunk for no good reason. My mom, on the other hand, was a workaholic, sometimes working three jobs at a time. That's how "love" looked in my house.

I'm the oldest and therefore the protector. My mother had me when she was fifteen and my siblings a couple of years later, all of us the biological children of the man who beat my precious mother. My little brother and sister would get in bed with me when my dad was on a rampage because they were scared. I snuggled with them under the covers and hid them.

Our house then was on Oakland Avenue, across the street from Franklin School, where we would eventually all attend. That house had stairs where I would sit and look through the rails, crying and asking God to stop my daddy from hitting my mommy. The beatings never stopped. My dad would come in the door drunk and start right in. Sometimes he brought friends over and beat my mom in front of them just to show off. He called her all kinds of names as he hit her, "bitch, bitch, bitch" being the least of it. When he was done, he'd pass out on the couch and sleep for hours.

I sat there on the stairs and wished him dead. I knew my mom was trying to shield us from what he was doing, but I saw it. All of it. She tried to stay strong during all that my dad was doing. It might have been easier if he forgot, but he remembered what he did. I knew because I heard him trying to apologize. I used to wonder why my mom didn't leave. As I grew a little older, I figured with my childhood logic that that's what love meant: hitting and apologizing, staying and accepting that apology.

Even when he wasn't home, I had a sense of dread because I didn't know when he was going to come back. But I knew what he was going to do to my mom when he got there. I lived on pins and needles and my mom did too, both of us trying to stay strong and protect each other.

Determination

My mother worked at factory jobs with three tiny children. Sometimes her mother watched us, sometimes we were in day care, and sometimes my dad watched us. My mom took a bus to work even though my dad had a car. To this day, I don't know why. That is the determination of a black mother.

I remember going to work with her sometimes; I'd sit on the dock while she worked her shift. Her last job was at Amway in the cosmetics department. My mom's work ethic is something to admire. Once I got out of the life and started working, I discovered I had inherited that work ethic. Nobody gave us anything; we worked for everything we got.

I was a tiny child, maybe four or five years old, when I remember seeing my mom lying on the couch. I'm not sure whether she was sick or my dad had beaten her so badly that she was in danger physically. He seemed to ignore her suffering, stretching the cord of our tan rotary phone as he talked to some friend. I pulled a chair over to the stove and turned it on, got out a pan, and filled it with milk. I heated the milk and brought it over to her to make her feel better. She'd done the same for me many times. She tried so hard to drink that foamy, warm milk.

My grandparents came through the door—I'm not sure why they stopped over—and took one look at her. They made my dad hang up and called an ambulance immediately. Mom was gone for several days for reasons she never explained to me.

Watching those beatings did something to me. I would sit in my bedroom holding my head in my hands because all I could hear was my mother's screams. How could she take those beatings and yet work as hard as she did every day? When she was at work, my dad had other women over to the house and beat them too!

One time I was upstairs in the attic, playing with my dolls while my brother and sister napped. I heard screams, ran down from the attic, and sat on the stairs. He had another woman in the house, beating her and holding her up against a wall.

Not long before my dad was arrested, I remember the one time my mom beat the crap out of him. He had hit her one too many times, and she whupped the dog snot out of him. When that happened, I felt a sigh of relief. He never hit her again, if you can believe that. My mother is a fighter. I didn't know she had hands like that.

I didn't realize how the dichotomy that was my father would affect so much of my life. I couldn't figure out how he could hit my mom and love her at the same time. How did love and violence live in the same house? Why didn't he hit us? And why did she stay with him when he hurt her? I know I loved and hated him at the same time. Perhaps she was afraid of him, or maybe she really did love him, this man who came from the South and settled in Grand Rapids, where she was born and raised.

Those questions about love and violence haunted me for years.

The violence stopped when my dad went to prison for killing a man in a dispute over another woman. He likely beat her too, based on what I'd seen him do. In any case, my mom divorced him while he was in prison, remarrying in the late 1970s when I was ten or eleven years old.

Love in Action, Not Words

My mom loved me and my younger brother and sister. She didn't say the words "I love you," but she showed us in lots of ways. She played flag football with us and some of the neighborhood kids in the Franklin School yard across the street from our house. She took us to the drive-in movies. She taught me how to sew; many a time

I watched her hunched over the sewing machine, Dippity-Do and big rollers in her hair, creating dresses and other clothing for us to wear. She made the majority of our clothes. Whatever we needed she made for us, because we didn't have money to buy clothes. My dad drank her money and his money, but she refused to go on food stamps. She worked hard to support us and did the best she could with what she had, and she kept us together.

She also taught me to cook; she'd be dead tired from working a couple of jobs one after the other, her feet hurting and her body aching, but she always let me watch her make a meal and gave me lessons along the way. She taught me how to cook from scratch, from cakes to meat loaf, from corn bread to fried chicken. Those smells comforted me, until my dad came home, anyway. Today I make similar food for my family, and those Southern soul-food smells still comfort me and make me remember the quality time with my mom.

We didn't receive hugs or words of love, but my mom made sure we had a home and clothing and food. That was her way of showing love. I found out years later that my mother couldn't give us the *I love yous* we craved. She couldn't give what she had never received. But I didn't realize then she couldn't say the words, and I missed it deep inside me. How could I miss what I didn't have? I couldn't put words to what I needed, but I knew I needed something.

My mom was tough when she had to be, especially after my dad went to prison. I was happy he was gone because I knew he couldn't hurt my mother anymore. I didn't miss him at all. Still, she took us to Jackson State Prison several times to visit him. I remember pulling up to that big old prison; I was afraid because it was so big. I looked to one side, and there was a cemetery for prisoners who had died and whose family never claimed their bodies. Those lines of white crosses were scary for a child to see.

We went in and had to give our names and be patted down before we saw my dad. He was sober and happy to see us, and we were happy to see him because I'd never seen him so loving and caring. He got out eventually but didn't live with us because by then my mom had divorced him and remarried.

One day, years later—I was in my early twenties—I was walking down Buckley Street toward Division, getting ready to work the Stroll. A brown Lincoln pulled past me, and all of a sudden I heard someone say, "Big Red!" Only one person called me that. I turned around and looked back. This man gets out of the Lincoln with a suit on, black shades, and a great big afro. He was standing there holding the car door so I didn't see the crutches.

I took off running toward him. It was my dad! I threw myself into his arms and he hugged me, then I got in the car with this man I had hated and loved. He knew I was on the streets, but he didn't say anything. We went riding around and talking about stuff with Uncle Sam, my dad's brother, who was with him.

"Popeye!" Uncle Sam said when he saw me, using the nickname he'd always called me. I hadn't seen him since I was little. He used to come and get me and take me to his house in Detroit. My dad would let me go with him without telling my mom. She'd get home and ask where I was at, and he'd say Detroit with Uncle Sam. He had a woman there with him, and she bought me all kinds of stuff, including a bike. She bought me whatever I wanted. Then my mother found out that the woman my uncle was with was not a woman. She had a fit, of course. But I remember that Uncle Sam loved me dearly.

After my mom remarried, she got into a fight with my stepfather's sister, for some reason. I mean a fight! The woman had come over to our house and got into it with Mom, but my little mama was throwing fists and really whupped her. The woman left but came back later with her family and busted out all of our windows. At that point my mom's parents, Nanny and PawPaw, got involved. Out came Granny's big ole pistol. Pretty soon all was calm on our street again. It was just another example of how my family came together when we had to.

Safe Places

When I was five years old, we moved to Oakland Avenue. My safe place during the violent times at home or when I'd had a rough day at school was the attic. It was a big space high above the drama. The attic was my sacred ground, my own little world, and no one could infiltrate my world.

I made the attic into my dollhouse, where I talked to my dolls about anything and everything. I could be quiet, think, process, or just forget what was going on in my life as I made up stories for my dolls. My favorite was Mrs. Beasley with her granny glasses and blue polka-dot dress; she was the favorite toy of the little girl Buffy on the television show *Family Affair*, which I loved to watch. When I pulled her string, she said the most calming things, things every child wanted to hear. I still remember what she said:

"Speak a little louder, dear, so Mrs. Beasley can hear you."

"If you were a little smaller, I could rock you to sleep."

"I do think you're the nicest little friend I ever had."

"If you could have three wishes, what would you wish for?"

"You may call me Mrs. Beasley. Would you like to play?"

I would respond to her, telling her how my day had gone, everything that happened to me, people who were mean to me. I told Mrs. Beasley about how I hated my father and how I thought the world should be. I created for her the perfect world through a child's eyes.

I loved that doll. Mrs. Beasley had an apron, so I would make myself aprons to match hers. I don't know what happened to my Mrs. Beasley from the attic, but years later after I was clean, my son stopped by my house one day with a package.

"This is from Grandma," he said.

I tore open the package and discovered an original Mrs. Beasley. My mom had bought me the doll I had loved so much. I burst into tears right then and there. I still have that beloved gift from my mom.

I also loved reading as a child, immersing myself in stories mostly involving princesses or heroines who found a prince or a best friend or a family. I loved stories with happy endings the very best; it's not hard to figure out why when I look back. I became Cinderella or Sleeping Beauty in my mind as I lived those fantasies, because they took me away from what was going on in my home.

We rarely played outside alone. When my mother went to work, I had to watch my little sister and brother, so having a childhood is something I know nothing about. We had bikes and toys, but it was hard to play like a child when I was taking care of and protecting my siblings. I had to become an adult real fast to help my mom. Yet I had the attic and my dolls and books.

Abuse in the Attic

In those days, my dad called me Big Red. I was a little girl living in a violent home, but I felt like my dad loved me in his own way. He was generous in some ways, like when he invited my much older cousin to live with us. "W" was probably in his late teens or early twenties when he moved in.

W took my siblings and me to the neighborhood store and bought us candy, played on the playground with us, and acted like he was trying to protect us when my dad beat my mom and went on his tirades. My cousin seemed to like me, spending time in the attic and playing dollhouse and Mrs. Beasley with me. He seemed so caring and kind. It was cool to have somebody to talk to, some form of human contact since my mom was always working and my dad was drunk.

One day I was in the attic talking to my dolls, telling them how I was feeling. They were my little therapists! My cousin came to play with me, which he'd done many times before, but this time something was different. He was watching me real strange. Then he slid into a little crawl space and pretended to be stuck, calling me to help him.

I went over to help, but he pulled me in there with him and started to touch me and talk about how special I was, saying how our time in the attic was our special time and not to tell anyone. He took my clothes off piece by piece, talking all the time and touching me. He raped me for the first time in that dusty attic.

As he penetrated me, I stared at a tiny hole in the corner of the roof. In my mind, that tiny hole got bigger and bigger until a rabbit came out and waved his little hand at me. He said, "Come here, Leslie. Run, run, run." In my head, I ran right into that little hole. Inside were children just like me. There was no blood; my father wasn't in there beating on my mother; no children were calling me names. There were children playing, lots of candy, and a feeling of happiness. It was the perfect world I had described for Mrs. Beasley. It was just me and children who were always there. There was no pain. We all looked alike; we all played together. Even Mrs. Beasley was there.

I was eight years old, a child surrounded by dolls and toys, lying on a dusty floor with a grown man on top of me.

"Don't tell, Leslie," he said. "If you say anything to anybody, your daddy will kill your mama. And that's the truth."

I nodded silently, tears streaming into my hair and my body aching with pain.

"You're not going to tell, are you?"

"No," I cried.

He crawled out of the small space, adjusted his clothing, and disappeared down the stairs.

I was scared and silent. I was afraid my parents would be angry with me if they found out what was going on. But I also knew that what he was doing was horribly wrong. He would let me know in subtle ways that he wanted to meet me in the attic. He would throw me signals with his eyes, jerk his head toward the stairs. I knew what he wanted and was too afraid to ignore him because I didn't want my mom to die.

I hid my siblings in a closet, not wanting them to experience the pain I was going through, and told them that when I got back, I'd buy them candy. Then I began the long journey up the stairs toward yet another rape by the cousin I called the bogeyman. Each time it happened, I stared at that tiny hole and went with my rabbit friend to a place of friendship and happiness.

The abuse went on for six or seven months, several times a week. I couldn't let anything happen to my siblings, and I didn't want my mom to die. I knew it was possible. The way my dad beat her, it sounded like he was killing her. I was terrified, yet I hid it well. But I couldn't hide everything.

The only time I saw my dad throw away his crutches was the day he opened the door to the bathroom and found me cleaning up the blood running down my legs with towels I would later hide or throw away. He hadn't realized I was in there. My eyes were big as saucers as he stared down at me.

"Big Red," he said. His only words.

I was terrified he'd be mad at me, but I saw his mind begin working. My actions in the bathroom alarmed him, so I tried to cover up. His face slowly turned to rage. I knew for sure he was going to kill my mother.

Crash went the crutches. He ran into his bedroom and rustled around. Then he pounded up the stairs three or four at a time, yelling at the top of his lungs. I heard my father arguing and screaming, my cousin pleading. I don't know what they said exactly, but I sure heard the gunshot. I was terrified; I didn't know what was going on. Had W killed my dad?

What happened was my dad had grabbed one of the many guns around our home and aimed it at my cousin, intent on killing him. He missed; W took off, running for his life down the street.

Not one word was ever said about the shooting or the abuse. My mom had been at work when my dad discovered me in the bathroom, so she didn't know a thing. My siblings never said a word about Daddy shooting at W, and I never said anything about the molestation. I finally told my mom decades later, after I got clean. It was just another thing we didn't talk about at my house.

I didn't see W again until my dad's funeral when I was in my twenties. I found out later he had abused a number of my cousins as well. As deep as I thought I'd buried the abuse, when I saw him at the funeral all those years later, I went livid with rage. My rape at the hands of a trusted adult came rushing back to the surface, and I was again that terrified, terrorized child. I felt the fear, the pain, the shame all over again. It took me months to recover from seeing him.

My cousin died a couple of years ago. I did not mourn his passing even for a second.

When his sister texted me and told he had died, all I could say was "Good." I later apologized to my cousin; it was her brother and she still loved him, and I should have had a little empathy for her, though I had none for him.

School Days

School was tough for me, but not because I couldn't do the work. In fact, I did very well in school. I was highly intelligent, read all the time, and completed all my schoolwork. There was nothing more they could teach me at my grade level, so the teachers wanted to move me up a grade. My mother said no, so they transferred me to Blandford School, a sixth-grade school for gifted children.

This was a nature-based school that had mostly white city kids learning to do things like make butter and tap maple trees.

I enjoyed my year there, but the focus on the natural world didn't prevent my restlessness. I often immersed myself in books, reading book after book to help anesthetize myself in the midst of the drama that was my home. I did homework the minute I got it, finishing it quickly and often early so I could return to my books.

I couldn't hide from myself, though. In hindsight, I realize now I could have had ADHD. In those days in inner-city schools with little funding and inadequate services, learning disabilities often remained undiagnosed. I understood the work easily, but it took a lot of concentration to get it done. I focused on schooling because if I didn't, the pain, voices, blood, and screams took over my mind and hit me all at once. I didn't know what to do with them.

I felt like I was a pressure cooker waiting to explode. Every beating I saw my dad give to my mom, every time I was raped, every time I felt the cruelty of other children added to the load of trauma I carried. Every day, I brought that trauma to school. Is it any surprise I retreated into books and homework, no matter how hard it was to concentrate? Those things grounded me amid the chaos of life.

Once I got to middle school, trauma and PTSD got the better of me. I started on a long journey to pregnancy, prostitution, and addiction.

As I look back, I sometimes wonder what God had in mind. My childhood wasn't peaceful, safe, or calm as I experienced trauma after trauma. Yet I also see God's hand. My mother loved me, showing it through actions and daily care. We went to church often; Gospel Temple Baptist Church was right next door. It felt like I could hear the choir practicing or performing old Negro hymns through the open church windows every time something bad happened. Almost by osmosis, I soaked in the words and messages of those songs and sermons that drifted through the windows. Little did I know I would later come to rely on those long-held memories as I came back to the God who held me in his tender, loving hands as I entered a dark, dark world.

Dear Reader,

A person's past trauma—childhood sexual abuse, violence, addictions, unplanned pregnancies, accidents, deaths, and much more—informs their present life and can't be ignored. Understanding and assisting them in learning how to heal from those traumas must happen before a new life really begins.

Whether you are a licensed professional or a layperson, understanding the impact of trauma is absolutely necessary. Laypeople can get training in the rudiments, but leave the hard work of trauma therapy to professionals.

Please know that every person is more than their past. One of the most important things to grasp is that while the past may inform the present, it doesn't have to control it. God will redeem any person's past for their good and, as he did with mine, for the good of others.

Each of us is a precious treasure to God. Each of us can find freedom. God wants freedom for all of us! He wants it for you.

Love, Leslie

Join the Revolt

1. Find a book, website, or blog to begin learning about trauma and its impact. There are many resources available that can start you on the path to knowledge about this important aspect of so many lives.
2. Look at the impact of trauma in your own life. What have you experienced? What experiences have you buried for

so long that might now be considered trauma? How has trauma in other people's lives, such as a parent or spouse, impacted your life?

3. Begin praying for women who have experienced trauma, for prostituted women in particular, and for God to mold your attitude and assumptions appropriately regarding these women.

4. Connect with a ministry such as Sacred Beginnings in Grand Rapids, Michigan, that works with prostituted women by first visiting its website (www.sbtp.org) and learning more about the ministry. Look for a ministry in your area as a place to start.

5. If you work in health care or education, consider how trauma may impact your patients and students. If you work in a church or parachurch ministry, how might knowledge of trauma impact your sermons, teaching opportunities, and counseling?

Chapter 2

THE PROCESS

As far back as I can remember, I was a child with no place in the world, and that, along with not knowing what real love was, made me vulnerable. Since the '60s, my neighborhood was predominantly African American, but I was light-haired and very light-skinned. The student body at my school was majority African American, with some Latinos and a few Caucasian kids. My hair was curly like my siblings' hair, but blonde, unlike my African American peers. Yet it wasn't straight enough for me to fit in with the white community. The white children at school knew I wasn't like them based on the texture of my hair alone.

The kids called me Heinz 57, Oreo, and mutt. I was always on the outside looking in at church, in school, and in the neighborhood.

This outsideness crept into my soul, making me feel alienated. I didn't have anyone who understood me. I wanted a friend, someone I could talk to and play with, but because I looked so different, no one wanted to play with me. All my life I was alone, and that eventually made me an easier target for a predator. It started with all that name-calling, but quickly got worse.

I remember being on the teeter-totters at Franklin Elementary when I was pushed off by a couple of girls calling me "honky" and "white girl." One girl was in my class and one was a little older. They said I didn't have any business being there, that they'd wait for me after school to beat me up. When the final buzzer rang, we exited out the back of the school. My house was across from the front of the school, so I had to walk around.

They caught me as I walked out the back door and pushed me around and called me names. This went on almost every day for weeks. I was scared to go to school, scared to go to sleep at night. I knew when I got to school, those girls would be there, grabbing my hair and jumping on me. When I was at school, I kept to myself, reading books and trying to stay in for recess. It was a really lonely feeling, sitting there by myself and watching everyone else play and talk to their friends. I had no one.

One day I ran home from school because one of the girls was trying to beat me up. My mother came out on the porch that day because she was tired of me being bullied and running home from school scared.

"You either fight her or you fight me," she said from the porch step, staring hard.

As many whuppings as my mother had given me, I knew I wasn't going to fight her.

I was petrified to fight that girl, but I was more afraid of what my mama was going to do if I didn't fight back.

I jumped on her and began hitting her, and I lost my mind. Weeks and weeks of bullying and name-calling came out in my fists. Naturally our brawl brought all the neighborhood kids around to watch and comment. Somebody must have told her mom, because pretty soon she came running down the street. Boy, did she and my mama have words.

"Every time your daughter comes around here to fight with my daughter, she'll be ready," my mom said.

And I was, from that moment on.

Whoever messed with me, hit me, called me names, or picked on me got my fist in their face. I didn't take anything from anyone anymore. Yet as I trudged home from school to another afternoon of caring for my siblings and perhaps another rape, I felt like I wasn't part of the world I lived in. I didn't belong. If there was an upside to my cousin living with us, it was that there were fewer fights. He wouldn't let us fight and was always there watching.

Once I fought that neighborhood bully, I thought school might change for me. It was supposed to be a place where children got along and teachers made sure everything was going to be OK. But it wasn't that way for me even when the fights stopped. Beating that girl didn't make me one of them.

School was one more place of pain—physical pain, but also mental and emotional pain from not being accepted, being called horrible names. I was still alone. I had no one else to rely on.

Change and Routine

After my dad ran off my cousin with curses and a gunshot, our lives continued as if nothing had happened. I went back to church for a while because a neighbor, Mrs. Rostic, stopped me one day and asked me to go to Sunday school. I did, but I was angry with God because horrible things continued to happen. In my mind, God wasn't real because a real God would never allow bad things to happen to children. All the talk about Jesus protecting little children didn't make sense to me. Don't get me wrong. I wanted to believe it, wanted it to be true. It just didn't fit what I saw, and that left me hurt. Instead of giving me a place to run to, it left me on the outside once again.

My mother was always working and my father was always drunk or gone, though he sure had money for the new cars he always brought home. I didn't know where he got that money. While I took care of my younger brother and sister at home, I wondered why I looked so different from them, but it wasn't something I could talk to my mom about. I was afraid to ask because the only form of communication in my house was screaming, yelling, and cussing. I kept quiet. Whatever was behind my differences, I felt them in my bones and heart every day.

One day when I was nine or ten, the police came and surrounded our house. I had never seen so many police with guns drawn. Once they had the house surrounded, they came in and got my dad. They handcuffed him and took him away to jail. We stood there crying, not understanding why they took our dad. But we learned soon enough. He had shot and killed a man over a white woman.

The next day I was terrified to go to school because my father had killed somebody else's dad. Turns out I was right: we had to face the children who had lost their father because of our dad. I thought I might have to fight them, but I didn't. Those kids were hurting too bad to worry about me.

For a little girl who was already terrified of life, I didn't need this too. We couldn't go outside and play for a while because that man's family lived in the same neighborhood. But my mother kept her head held high and continued to care for me, my sister, and my brother. The memory of her rising above the chaos surrounding my father is etched in my mind forever.

I also remember helping my mom clean out the house after my dad was gone. I found guns everywhere, plus pills and marijuana hidden in nooks and crannies all over the house. I knew about the alcohol, but not about the dope. In fact, I didn't know what dope was, but I knew that what was in my hand shouldn't have been there.

I was confused about the secrets I had to keep. I was different, I was changed, I was less than, I was lost. Worse, there was no one to help me. I had feelings and emotions that I didn't know were feelings and emotions. They came from every side, hitting me all at once.

One time before he was arrested, my father woke me out of a sound sleep and put me on his lap. We had an old record player, and he was playing "United We Stand" by Brotherhood of Man. We always had music playing on the record player or on the radio, so I wasn't put off by the music. My dad was holding me real tight. I don't know why he did that, but I think about that moment often. It was so out of character for him to show me any kind of affection; I didn't know what to do with it.

It was normal for me to be uncertain about so many things in my life, afraid of anything and everything, and nervous of what was going to happen next.

Becoming Who I Needed to Be

One of the hardest shocks occurred when my mom and the school transferred me to Blandford School, a predominately white school for gifted students. When I got off the bus on the first day of sixth grade, a little white girl said, all proper and in a dialect I barely understood, "Hi! My name is Amy." I was afraid and shocked, but I immediately put on another mask and said just as properly, "Hi! My name is Leslie. How are you?"

That school was a culture shock for me. The language was different, the dialect was different, the learning was different. Once again I was in a situation where I was forced to act a certain way to fit in. But because I wore so many masks just to get through the days, I picked up on it all really quickly. I was one person at school, but the minute I stepped off the bus at home, I went back to what I knew in my hood. Then I'd go back to school and speak their language and act like they did. This went on for the entire school year.

I just wanted to belong. But deep inside, I knew I didn't. I asked myself why I wasn't just black. Was I also white, Puerto Rican, Indian? Why was I raped? Why was I hurt? Why all this pain? Why was I different?

To compensate, I became whoever I needed to be in the moment. That was the beginning of wearing many masks. If I needed to fight, I fought. If I needed to be a parent to my siblings due to my mother working so many jobs to care for us, I became that parent to my siblings.

I asked myself every day, Why me? Why did I have such a jacked-up family? Why was I biracial? Why didn't I look like everybody else? Why was I always on the outside looking in? The need to fit in taught me how to wear so many masks, but even I didn't know who I was. It was like I was standing on the outside of myself looking in. I was always trying to be who others wanted me to be in order to not be left out, so I never even knew *me*.

Acting Out

I got quite heavy, eating everything in sight to hide my fears. I figured that if I got heavy, people wouldn't hurt me anymore because I was unattractive. They would leave me alone.

I was nine or ten years old when my dad went to prison. I ate, I hid, I hated. A couple of years later, my mom remarried. Because I was so mixed up and confused, I didn't like my stepdad because he wasn't my dad, whom I loved and hated all at the same time.

By then I was a young adolescent, and I acted out like many adolescents do, especially ones who have been raped and lived in dysfunctional families. I became promiscuous, not understanding I was looking for the love I had never received from my father. Boys told me I was pretty and that they liked me, and that validated my need for acceptance. I looked for love and acceptance from the boys in the neighborhood the only way I knew how. I got pregnant at age fourteen.

My mom was a force to be reckoned with, so I was terrified to tell her I was pregnant. I told her as I stood in the doorway, one foot in the house and one foot outside in case I needed to run. She was upset, of course, but also mad as hell. I chose to have an abortion at the clinic on Cherry Street.

I remember the pain. I lay there on the cold, sterile table in so much pain. Turns out they ruptured my uterus, and I had to be rushed to the hospital in an ambulance. Emergency surgery followed because some of the baby was still inside me. I cry thinking about it to this day. Because of that abortion, having a C-section was the only safe way for me to deliver a baby from then on.

I hated school, but I was on the drill team through the ROTC and I loved spinning those rifles. I loved being a pom-pom girl because I could dance really well. My mom had taught us to dance and roller-skate. But I was still on the outside looking in: I was heavy and they were skinny; they were popular girls and I wasn't.

The father of my second child was someone from school. He was older than me, and he was also in ROTC, which I thought was cool. He said he liked me and asked me out to a school dance. I was shocked and excited and giddy, because someone like him had asked out someone like me. My mom got me a pretty light-green dress for the dance, and he came to the door in his ROTC uniform. We had a good time at the dance, and I started seeing him more and more. At school, we would have lunch together and we would talk. We'd sneak into my house when my mom was at work to have sex. We'd also use the camper parked in the backyard.

My mom was hurt and angry at my second pregnancy when I was fifteen, not understanding what caused me to do this again. I always wanted something I could love unreservedly and that would love me back like Mrs. Beasley did. A baby seemed like the answer. Of course I couldn't tell her about the rapes. I'd kept the secrets of my childhood—the beatings, the sexual abuse, the screams coming from my mom, the fact that I couldn't prevent any of it. Little did I know all that trauma was affecting me mentally, emotionally, spiritually, and physically.

The birth of my son changed me. I loved my son, but I still didn't love me. I didn't know what it took to take care of a baby, which was obviously more complicated than taking care of my dolls. I continued to go to school while my mom cared for him or brought him to day care, and I continued in ROTC. I came home each day to take care of my son. Yet the voices didn't stop; the nightmares didn't stop. The voices just became louder and louder, and the memories were more vivid and real. Every time I closed my eyes to go to sleep, I'd see and hear the violence of my early childhood and the houses where we'd lived. After my mom remarried, she moved out of the house where I was raped to Calvin Street, but no place was safe to me. Everywhere I went, I felt and saw the same things.

I felt like I had to run. I ran away from home and ran away from school, though I didn't know what I was running from or what I was running to. I just knew I needed to go. I felt like a combustion engine running on high, about to blow. Each time I ran, the police picked me up and my mom came and got me. I would stay awhile before the memories and the voices became louder and louder, and once again I would run, like I was trying to run out of my skin. I would leave my son with my mom and disappear for a couple of days until the police brought me home.

My mother began taking me to a therapist, but that didn't work. First off, he was a man. He started by asking me questions, but I didn't answer him because I didn't trust him—or anyone, for that matter. The people I trusted to love and care for me didn't, so what would make him any different?

He didn't talk with me; he talked at me. I remember walking into his office for the first time and seeing this huge desk. That desk, with him behind it, was menacing to me. He had one of those lounge couches where he tried all this weird therapy stuff on patients, but not on me. When he asked me to lie on that couch, I completely lost it. I began raging and screaming and tearing up his office, enough that they called the guards and locked me up once again in juvenile detention. I was so filled with hate and rage. Looking back, I was terrified and fighting the officers because I didn't understand why they were locking me up.

I started stealing as well, first little stuff from the candy store, but then I'd run away from school or home and go with my friends to bigger stores and steal clothes and makeup, once again just to fit in. We got caught some of the time, but often we didn't. I was rebelling and acting like a fool. I hung out with a crowd that was just like me: angry, rebellious outsiders who didn't feel like they belonged anywhere.

One day I stole a bunch of money from a friend's mother and ran away again. I was pretty filled out for being only fifteen, so I looked older. I didn't have any place to go, so I roamed the streets until I happened to see a For Rent sign in the window of a house that had been divided into lots of apartments. A man was going into the building with painting supplies. I started talking to him and found out he owned the building. I looked in the window of the first-floor apartment in the back and saw its one bedroom, little living room, kitchen, and bathroom. It looked like a dollhouse to me, and I loved it immediately. He rented me the apartment right away with no questions asked. He never asked for an ID, my age, how I would pay the rent, and whether I had a job. He saw the money and that was all he cared about.

My plan was to take my son from my mom's house and live with him in this apartment. And that's what I did. Here I was, a fifteen-year-old with an infant and an apartment near the corner of Sheldon Avenue and Logan Street. I had no form of income and no clue how to live on my own.

I used to sit on my little front porch with my son and watch women jumping in and out of cars along the street. I had no idea what was going on or the dangers that lurked there. I had no understanding of how close I was to and how deep I would fall into the darkness.

Living in the Darkness

The darkness doesn't ask questions; it just accepts you and validates you . . . at least at first. That darkness is where I found myself a lot of the time, walking down the street at night and crying in anger, frustration, fear, desperation, and confusion. A friend watched my son as I walked in that darkness, a young girl with no guidance, alone, trying to figure myself out. That place is where he found me.

He pulled up alongside me in his big car and spoke to me. "Why are you crying? Are you OK?"

I said nothing.

"C'mon, let me take you out to eat, because you've got no business being out here alone," he said.

I got in the car. Once I opened that door, my life took a turn. Little did I know what was in store for me.

He took me to a place to eat, asking me why I was crying and about my family. He stared at me at first, then started talking to me like he really cared. I relaxed because I felt no fear.

When I think back to his questions and how he asked them, I now understand he was gaining information from me to manipulate my thought processes and turn me against my family for his benefit.

He told me that he couldn't figure out why someone would do this or that to me, that I was beautiful, that if he'd been there, he would have done this and that to that person. It was everything I needed to hear. It made me feel heard, accepted, protected, and not alone. Afterward, he took me back to my friend's house, where I was staying since I didn't want my mom to find me at my own apartment. He and I arranged to meet again at my friend's house. He took me out to eat and bought me clothes, which I kept at my friend's house, far from my mother's eyes. I saw him the next day and the next. He paid his sister to watch my son while we went out on the town.

"Your mother should have done this, shouldn't have done that. If she had done that, this wouldn't have happened to you," he said all the time. And I started to believe him. I started to get angrier and angrier with my mom and started to despise my family. I started to steal more often, and when I got caught, he would send his sister, who said she was my aunt, to come get me from the police station or juvenile detention. They let me go with no questions asked.

On our dates, we'd go to nice restaurants and events. We would drive up and down South Division Avenue, which I didn't know at the time was the Stroll, the Track. He talked all the time about how we were going to make money and do all kinds of wonderful things with that money. I didn't know how we'd get this money, but I agreed because this was my boyfriend and I believed at that time that he loved me.

After all, he took me to bars and clubs and introduced me to friends as his woman. If any man talked to me, he got upset; this showed me he loved me. He became my protector. We'd hit after-hours clubs when the bars closed, drinking and partying the nights away. Sometimes we went to his friends' homes after the bars closed. There was so much wining and dining and shopping. This was a world I knew little about, but before long I loved the attention I received from him and liked that I was protected by him. He came along like a knight in shining armor. He made me feel like a princess, just like the ones I'd read about in my books as a child.

He would ask me, however, to do things like shoplift, lie, or carry a gun for him just to see if I loved him. This was part of the game, part of the mind control he exercised over me. My need to fit in and feel loved and wanted fed right into his plan. The game is, once you get the mind, the body will follow.

This went on for maybe two months while I lived in that apartment with my son—clubbing, dating, testing, meeting his friends. What I didn't know was that all those men he took me to meet were also pimps. He was showboating me around. In my head he was showing me off because he loved me and cared about me. But in reality he was taking me around to other pimps to show them he had "knocked a bitch" (slang for "getting another ho").

One night we went to the house of one of his friends after the clubs closed, something we'd done many times before. This time, however, was much different. I passed out. Had I had too much to drink? Had he drugged me? I'll never know. What I do know is that when I woke up, his friend was on top of me having sex with me any way he wanted. I could only lie there in shock, unable to speak, unable to think. I looked up at the man who said he loved me and would never hurt me, hoping he'd stop this horrible event.

Instead, he looked at me like I was dirt under his shoe. He looked like the devil himself when he said, "Bitch, get my money."

I was only fifteen. I was crying, terrified, and like the little girl I was, all I wanted was my mom. But my life as a little girl was over.

Dear Reader,

So many prostituted individuals feel like they fit nowhere. They have adapted to that lack of identity by becoming whoever they need to be for the circumstances they are in. One of the best ways to help is to guide these individuals to experts who can help them find their true identity, the person they are in their deepest self. This isn't easy and is deeply personal, so please leave this tough work to experts in trauma therapy and other therapies. You, however, can help prostituted individuals by loving them where they are, regardless of their pasts. God loves each of us just as we are, and it is in that love that we all find our worth and our true selves.

You—and the people you come in contact with—may feel like you don't fit anywhere, but you fit in God's heart and in his plan for your life. To God, nothing—not the terrible things in your past, the things you regret, or the deepest secrets you want to hide—could change the deep love he has for you.

Love, Leslie

Join the Revolt

1. Research ministries to prostituted individuals in your area to find out how they are helping those who come to them. Are they using licensed therapists and social workers, among other professionals, as they provide help? Connect with those that do.

2. Create a list of well-vetted therapists, social workers, health-care workers, and clergy to whom you can refer individuals. Also create a list of ministries or programs you can connect them to regarding housing, employment, food, and other needs.

3. Do your own soul work to discover your true identity as a child of God. Seek out a therapist to assist you in that journey if needed.

4. Connect with people in your church or neighborhood who are interested in helping victims of prostitution. Talk about how you can work together to help these individuals, including assessing your strengths and resources.

5. Volunteer at a ministry or outreach to prostituted individuals to find out more about such work, whether you want to begin or stay in the work, and whether it's a fit with your strengths and desires, always making sure to check your motives.

Chapter 3

THE STROLL

My "boyfriend" immediately took me to a house located right off the Stroll. I never went back to my little apartment to live, only to clean out the place with "C" standing right there so I didn't run away. My infant son came to the house with me.

The Stroll, so conveniently close to the house where I now lived, was where women were prostituted every day and every night, where pimps controlled the streets, where police occasionally patrolled, where men came to pay for sex.

I and my wives-in-law lived with C in that house when we weren't on the Stroll. Maybe half a dozen of his women lived there at that time, and I was the youngest of the Stable, which is what they call it when a pimp has more than one person working for him. The "bottom bitch" is the pimp's number-one girl, tasked with over-seeing the rest of the girls. The bottom made sure that we met our quota every night and that we were dressed accordingly. She also made sure we didn't get "out of pocket" (out of line) while out on the Stroll or in the house.

I was terrified when C took me to that house after his friend had raped me. They didn't waste any time, that's for sure. The bottom and the other women gave me a drink and a Valium to calm me down, then did my makeup, put a wig on me, dressed me up, and drove me to the Track, another name for the Stroll. The bottom said, "If you run, if you tell the police, he will kill your mother, son, brother, and sister. Then he'll cut you up and spread your body parts across the state of Michigan." I believed every word she said.

I felt myself back in that place of panic, fear, and darkness. I couldn't do anything about what had happened to me and what was about to happen. I couldn't stop my cousin from raping me, I couldn't stop my dad from beating my mom, and I couldn't stop my "boyfriend" from forcing me into prostitution.

I realized almost immediately that he had lured me with his talk about money, going places, and doing things. He had made it all sound so exciting. He made me feel like I finally had a place to belong. I realized that the moment I opened his car door, I was alone and on the clock. I owed him for every meal he paid for, every outfit he bought me, every drink he gave me. I had to repay him with sex and the money I earned having sex with the men who came to the Stroll.

I was petrified the first time I stood on the Stroll, so soon after being raped and brought to the house. I watched four or five women standing on every corner, watched Cadillacs, Eldorados, and Lincolns cruise up and down the street, their drivers the pimps who controlled the women standing there. I watched as a trick pulled up to the corner and four or five women approached the car. He chose one, and off they went to someplace I didn't know. I watched the other girls on the corner and did what they did, putting my expertise at fitting in to "good" use.

I was only fifteen.

My first trick was an older, fat white man, who pulled up to me in a nice car. He looked at me, and the first thing he said was, "You must be new because I've never seen you out here before." I was scared half to death, not knowing what to say or do, so I just nodded. By this time I was feeling the effects of the Valium mixed with alcohol.

He quoted me a price of one hundred dollars "for some head and some sex." I got in the car and we drove to a hotel room on 28th Street right off Division Avenue. When we got in the room, he started taking off his clothes, but I just stood there. He handed me the money and was like, "C'mon, c'mon, c'mon." My hands were shaking as I got undressed. He lay across the bed, and I gave him a blow job until he got erect. I was so terrified. I put a condom on him, and this big, fat white man got on top of me and had sex with me any way he wanted to. When it was over, I was numb. I wasn't even of this world as I dressed and got back in the car. He dropped me off on the corner where I had been standing less than an hour before.

More women came to stand on the corner, and I started watching them to learn how the process worked. Every time a trick pulled up, four or five women walked up to the car window and talked to whoever was inside. It was like a bidding war with everybody talking at once, and he had the pick of whoever he wanted. He'd make his choice, she'd get in the car, and they would take off. I watched the older women who had more experience closely and learned well.

We didn't always go to hotel rooms to turn tricks. There was a house on Wealthy Street off of Eastern that was run by a much older lady. She rented rooms to women for five dollars a visit to turn their tricks. There were five bedrooms in that house. Each time you visited, you knocked on the door with your john. You went in, they would check you out, and if all was well, you paid them the five dollars, grabbed two washcloths, and went to the designated room. If the rooms were full, you waited outside until another pair came out and it was your turn. This brothel even sold condoms and sex toys at the door.

On Thursday, Friday, and Saturday nights, I could catch any-where from ten to fifteen to twenty tricks. Back then, South

Division was the hottest thing going. Money rolled in 24/7; the money didn't stop.

Johns sometimes took me to where they wanted to go, but the code on the streets was that you took them where you wanted to go, not the other way around. The reality was that if he took you where he wanted to go, he would rape you, beat you, and kill you, and you'd never be seen again.

I remember so much pain. Street prostitution is the darkest of the dark, and physical pain is part of that darkness. I got numb to the pain, numb to the knowledge that every time I got in a car, there was a fifty-fifty chance I wasn't coming back. I was so numb to having sex that it was an out-of-body experience.

Hang of the Game

It didn't take long before I got the hang of the game and became good at the hustle. I learned how to attract tricks; I learned the prices for various sex acts as well as the prices for time spent. I also learned how to make sure the trick wasn't the police. I learned how to clip a trick (steal from him). I was out there in the rain, sleet, blowing snow, and broiling heat, and on every holiday.

When I had been out on the Stroll for a while, I started getting regulars. Many of the men who picked me up wanted to talk. They rationalized and justified why they were doing this, talking to me about why they were there buying sex. They told me about their wives, about their fantasies and not being able to live them out with their wives so they had to come down and pick up a girl. I used to sit there waiting for them to get done talking about their issues and problems, thinking, *Hurry up and let's get this done. I'm not your sex therapist.*

I met sadomasochists, young boys, college boys, and old men, but the majority were white males. One guy used to drive up and down South Division wearing a diaper and a red ball gag tied around his mouth. He picked me up one day; all he wanted was for somebody to beat him, to actually whup him and call him a bad boy. Occasionally men would cry. They'd have sex with me and then cry, feeling all remorseful. *What the hell*, I thought.

I saw all ages and all walks of life. I saw people I recognized too. I was shocked sometimes at the people I saw. "I know you," I'd say. "What the f--- you doing down here?" They never had a good answer.

Sometimes women came and bought sex. Late one night, a big motor home came down the street, turned a corner, and came back up Pleasant Street, where the driver parked and shut off the lights. That lets you know a john wants to talk to you. I went over and got in and sat there talking to a person wearing a white baseball cap. I thought it was a man, but when I looked closely, I discovered it was a female. I got right up out of there. That was not my thing. I was amazed at husbands and wives who approached me together, wanting a threesome. It's not just men out there. There are all sorts.

Family Gets Involved

My mom soon found out where I was and what I was doing. She came and got my son from the house, eventually getting full custody of him. I was hurt, but I knew this was best for my baby. From that point on, I realized the best love I could give to my children was to give them to someone who could care for them. I love each of my babies. I was made by my pimp to have more abortions than I can count.

My mom and grandmother and aunts would come to South Division Avenue looking for me. When they saw me, they'd jump out of their cars and try to chase me down. But I'd take off running, escaping into the dark alleys and streets that I knew all too well. What they didn't know was that I longed to run toward them. I wanted to be back home with my mom, safe once again. But I knew I had to run away from them to save their lives. They only saw a headstrong, troubled girl who was bent on ruining her life. I knew that if I left, C would find them and hurt every one of them.

Occasionally the police picked me up for a curfew violation, taking me off the corner and straight to juvenile detention, where they knew me well. My pimp would send his sister to get me out, then hide me for a day or two. But I was back on the Stroll as soon as possible. One time I was put into juvenile detention and I "knocked a bitch." I talked another girl into the life, and I did that for my pimp's love and acceptance. All I wanted him to do was love me; all I wanted was to be accepted, just like I had wanted and needed when I was a child. So I knocked that girl, not knowing or understanding that it would ruin her life.

I remember as a child giving other kids my milk money to be my friend. I was again to that point in my mind, thinking that making this man happy would make me accepted. I thought I could buy his love by doing what he asked me to do. Not doing what he wanted meant that I got beat to within an inch of my life. I wanted him to be happy and proud and not to beat me.

I lost a lot of weight during this time. Of course I did! I was walking up and down South Division night after night, working the circuit (traveling from state to state), walking to most places I needed to go, walking and walking and walking. This is part of the life of prostitution: always hustling, never stopping. Always trying to walk away from the darkness inside myself.

Becoming Candy

I knew I couldn't escape or just leave, so I acclimated myself to the lifestyle. After all, I was good at becoming who I needed to be when I needed to be them. There was Little Leslie, the wounded child who couldn't protect herself, her siblings, or her mother from the beatings. There was Big Leslie, the fighter who would go to any lengths to protect those she loved, though she was most often protecting Little Leslie. And there was Candy. Candy was my working name, and every time I went to the Stroll, Candy appeared. Nobody went by their real names on the Stroll—we chose names or our pimp gave us names. With Candy came power and control.

I'd been called names and mistreated because of being biracial, but as Big Leslie or Candy, I was powerful. I was strong and the cutest thing around, the baddest bitch going. I was surviving on the streets, using alcohol and sneaking Valium and yellow jackets to avoid thinking and feeling. Everybody I knew out on the streets was on something. We had to be in order to survive the physical and emotional trauma.

Prostitution in the 1980s was all about power and control. Turning into Candy every night gave me both. Whatever I asked a man to spend, he'd spend on me. Whatever I asked him to pay, he'd pay. My mind adapted to the trauma I faced every day so I could survive. This gave me a false sense of self-esteem and self-worth. When I wasn't Candy—when I was Little Leslie—I was alone and afraid. Candy took care of Leslie.

I lived with so much trauma that I existed on a hair trigger. At any given moment I knew where to go and what to do to escape. I sat with my back against the wall so I could see everything coming my way. I was hypervigilant all the time, always questioning people's motives. I knew everyone had a motive, whether it was good or bad. In my world then and now, people have to go above and beyond to prove themselves because I expect the worst. I expect the worst because the worst has always happened to me.

I operated out of fear and the need to be needed. I did whatever I could to keep the pimp happy, because if I didn't, he beat me. If I didn't make my quota or he felt like I was out of pocket, he'd come after me. I've been beaten with sticks, belts, hangers—one time a bat. If he found me or the other women at the Acapulco Restaurant getting something to eat or a cup of coffee, we'd better have the money or we'd get beat right there. He'd slap us, stomp on us, or drag us outside and beat us on the street.

When I first started on the Stroll, we weren't allowed to get high. Pimps weren't handing out hard drugs because being out there high wasn't good for business. We could go have a drink or something to eat, but as soon as we were done, we had to get back out on that corner.

There was a lot of rape. I know, it's counterintuitive to think a prostituted woman could be raped, but it happens all the time. Men did things we didn't want them to do, refused to pay, beat us, threw us out of their cars when they were done. They treated us like faceless, voiceless nothings.

I was held hostage, beaten, forced to turn tricks in horrible weather, and I had to have sex with the pimp whenever he wanted. Yet day after day, month after month, year after year, I went right back into the darkness no matter what brutal situation I had come out of, because such things were part of the job. I had to fool myself into believing these things wouldn't happen again, that I would do things different. Survival was all I could think about, except for those times when the pimp acted like he loved me.

A lot of times when I made my quota, he'd pick me up and be so pleased with me. He'd tell me how much he loved me, that I didn't have to go out that night and could be with him instead. "Get dressed," he'd say, "we're going out." He did this with all the girls who lived in that house, and we all looked forward to our special nights with C. Whoever made the most money got to go with him.

As I look back now, I realize I was likely experiencing Stockholm syndrome. I was held hostage and mistreated by this man, yet I loved my abuser. I remember seeing him shed a tear when I was sentenced to jail time for prostitution. I thought that meant he truly cared about me, but he was probably crying because he was losing money with me in jail.

After many of the beatings, he told me he did it for my own good so I wouldn't do this or that again, or that I'd caused him to beat me because of something I had done. He almost always told me the reason for the beating or other punishment, and I believed him every time. I remember watching my father beat my mother viciously and then telling her that he loved her, and she never left him. So when my pimp beat me, I believed he loved me because of what I'd seen as a child.

He also told me that he was the only one who loved me, that my family didn't love me, because if they did, then they wouldn't have done this and that when I was younger. My mind was so backward then, thinking that the man who beat me really loved me and that my family, who repeatedly tried to rescue me, didn't.

I was deep in the darkness, and that darkness accepted me and asked no questions. I worked in the darkness and came to see it as a haven, my safe place. I came to see prostitution as power and control. I came to see it as a place with no way out, so I acclimated to the lifestyle so I could survive in my own mind.

Trying to Save My Life

I can't even count how many times I was arrested. I've been in and out of institutions—juvenile detention and jail—all my life. I would be arrested for prostitution and spend time in jail, then go right back to what I knew.

When I was sentenced to jail time in the early days, my mom came to see me. But she soon discovered I wasn't changed and started to visit less. Still, at one point when I ended up back in jail, my mom visited. She sat there looking at me through a glass partition, a scarf wrapped around her head. She pulled the scarf off to reveal her bald head, with only one strand of hair. She was going through chemo for breast cancer and I didn't even know. I was so ashamed, so hurt. My mama could have died and I wouldn't have known a thing about it. I was so deep in the darkness that my family couldn't find me and I couldn't find them. Once, my mother and stepfather drove by me and I took off running, not knowing that that very day my mother was going for chemotherapy.

My brother and sister came looking for me as well. It terrified me to see them and that they knew I was out there like that. I felt like I had abandoned them. They had looked up to me and I had taken care of them and protected them, but I left them. To this day, my leaving them still messes with me, but we have a strong relationship now, and I'm back to being the big sister they love and need.

I was busy getting high when my father was in the hospital after a massive heart attack. He was dying and my family was looking for me. They found me high in a hotel. My siblings really needed me to be there with them, but in the mindset I was in, I was mentally and emotionally unable to. My father passed away, and I went to his funeral. I froze when I saw my cousin there. I didn't speak to him then, but I got really angry and wanted to hurt him like he'd hurt me, but the funeral wasn't the place and time. At the repast (where everyone goes to eat after the funeral), he was talking to me like nothing ever happened. I looked at him with so much hate and said, "I remember." My mother saw the interaction between my cousin and me, and I could see the question mark on her face, but I still didn't tell her.

The little girl who had been raped and abused was there at first, but Big Leslie popped up and was ready to fight. Something in my cousin's face told me he knew I wanted to kill him, and he got away from me real quick. I wasn't that little vulnerable girl anymore, not at all. I was no longer afraid. I was strong enough to beat his ass, but I didn't get the chance.

I didn't know what fun was. Fun to me was going to the bars and not having to go to work. As a child I read and played with dolls to escape, but on the streets I used alcohol and pills as an escape.

Instead of the fantasies of my childhood, I escaped deeper into the darkness.

Deep in the Life

Downtown Grand Rapids in the 1980s was full of bars, Mexican restaurants, and gas stations. Steketee's Department Store, Langdon's Lounge, Wepman's Pawnshop, and the Herkimer Hotel were still operating then. Kleinman's Menswear outfitted all the pimps with their flashy shirts and shoes. People were everywhere— shopping, going to and from work, visiting restaurants and bars. There were also four or five girls on every corner from Fulton Street on the north to 28th Street on the south. Eldorados, Mercedeses, and Lincolns from out of state cruised the Stroll, driven by pimps in expensive suits.

Violence abounded as well. Pimps jumped out of those fancy cars and beat the women. They used hangers and bats, and dragged the girls across the sidewalk. Sometimes a pimp made his girls jump on other girls, and if they didn't he'd beat them too. The Stroll was a world unto itself, with the pimps in charge. The police had a presence, but that presence didn't change much about life on the streets. There were even policewomen who occasionally dressed up and stood out on the corners to arrest johns. The fear of arrest never stopped the men from coming around.

On the streets, you either grow up or die. I lived at animal level, struggling to survive. The darkness is something you learn to navigate like the back of your hand. You become so addicted to the lifestyle that it soaks into every fiber of your being. You live and breathe the streets, with the violence and darkness and chaos and hustle and bustle of the night life. You learn how to accept it. You accept it or you die.

I entertained thoughts about leaving, but I didn't know what I would do instead. I didn't know what the other side of the darkness was like. Out there in the other world, I had only experienced people judging, objectifying, dehumanizing, and making me feel voiceless and faceless. People see the effects of prostitution, but they don't take the time to understand the causes. It's easier to point fingers and call people names rather than know them. I had wanted to be a nurse or a doctor when I was child. I even wanted to be Cher! I always wondered what life was like outside of my family unit, but I never got a chance to find out before I was taken by C.

The South Division Avenue of the 1980s was the heart of downtown and the heartbeat of the prostitution world. When crack cocaine came on the scene, however, South Division spun in a downward spiral and soon became a crack haven.

Dear Reader,

Beatings, rape, and other forms of abuse are not love, no matter where you live. The people in your life who say and do otherwise are wrong and do not love you. Love doesn't hurt, whether you live in the suburbs or the inner city. God's love is unending, without limit, and without pain. He offers it to you freely, without payment or excuses or "extras." He loves you extravagantly and always will.

Prostituted individuals, as well as those who have been abused in other ways, may experience a form of Stockholm syndrome, a coping mechanism in which they have positive feelings toward the abuser and may even protect him or her. Psychotherapy with a trusted clinician can help. If you suspect Stockholm syndrome, encourage those individuals to seek help.

Also know that the things I describe in this chapter don't just happen someplace else. They happen in your town, in your city, and sometimes in your neighborhood. The tragedy of trafficking is in your backyard.

The darkness is all-encompassing. For people who live in that dark world, the light is foreign; the light is dangerous and frightening. You, however, can begin to be that light for those who live in the darkness. Love these individuals without judgment, and let your light shine on them.

Love, Leslie

Join the Revolt

1. If you are working with people who have been trafficked, talk to them gently about which events in this book or in their lives might trigger them. Take care to avoid triggering words, questions, noises, or physical contact.
2. Research the causes and effects of trafficking to find out how it affects the minds of those held against their wills, and make yourself aware of common words and phrases a prostituted individual might say.
3. Close your eyes for one minute—enough time to get used to the darkness. Now open them and feel how the light constricts your pupils. Imagine how it feels to live in physical and spiritual darkness and suddenly be exposed to the light.
4. Research starting a ministry through your church that offers personal hygiene items such as bodywash, shampoo, toothbrushes, toothpaste, feminine care products, lip balm, combs, and brushes, as well as small food items such as energy bars. Also research a ministry that will accept these items and get them to women in need.
5. Start a prayer group that focuses on trafficked individuals. Pray specifically for their safety, mental health, spiritual health, self-esteem, and physical health.

Chapter 4

STAYING

I had power over men. They wanted me, wanted to pay me for what I could give them. They did what I wanted them to do because they wanted me. There was so much power in that transaction for me, the little girl who had no power over the cousin who raped her or the kids at school who bullied and talked about her—no power over anything that happened to her. I realize now I was never in control; God was always in control, because by "man's law" I should be dead.

Sometimes I lost power and situations became deadly; it wasn't uncommon for me to be raped and/or beaten by a trick. He wanted the sex but didn't want to pay for it, so he would overpower me and take what he wanted. That's rape. Sometimes a john would take me way out of the neighborhood and then shove me out of the car when he was done raping me. I remember a john beating me and taking his money back, then leaving me far away from Grand Rapids. The rain came down in sheets as I trudged through areas I didn't know, crying and asking God, *Why?* Someone eventually picked me up, but when I got home, I was beaten by my pimp because I came back with no money. That night I had to stay out longer than usual until I made back my quota.

Another deadly situation was the time I was held hostage, tied up in a basement with my arms above my head. The john had jimmied the door of his car so I couldn't get out and then held a pistol to my head. The ride seemed to take forever before he dragged me out of the car and into a dark basement.

I was beaten and raped repeatedly, violated with a variety of objects. He threatened to mutilate and kill me, and I believed him. He beat me until I passed out. I slumped down again and again over the course of several days, eventually loosening the ropes that held my hands. Despite all the threats and terror, I worked myself free, then tried to find a way out of the basement. He had covered the windows with wood, but I was able to yank down the wood and unlatch a window. I crawled out, covered in blood and filth. The woman who lived next door saw me and screamed, then wrapped my naked body in a blanket and called the police. The john ran for his life and was never caught, much less prosecuted. I went back to work a week later after having said no to a request to go to the hospital. Hospitals were places of pain and humiliation.

My life was in jeopardy almost daily. I was at the Gateway Motel with a john one night just after leaving the Limelight, where I had been drinking and taking pills. I was passed out on the bed, but I heard a voice yell, "Move!"

I jerked awake and leaped out of bed and hit the wall. That john was coming after me with a machete! It was either fight or flight and I couldn't run, so I had to fight. I turned around and grabbed a chair and hit him with it as he came at me. Somehow I got to the door and got away, but I still have a scar on my leg from where he got a piece of me with that machete.

Many women have died in motels at the hands of johns, and I would have been one of them that day had I not had the super-human strength that comes with so much fear. I didn't report the incident, because the first time I reported something to the police I was treated and looked at like dirt. Years later, my mom and I were talking about my Aunt Shasta, my mother's sister who had passed away years earlier, and it hit me like a ton of bricks that the voice I heard in that motel room that yelled "Move!" was my Aunt Shasta's. She, somehow, saved my life.

These are the kinds of things that happen out there on the streets. We are beaten, stabbed, robbed, raped, disparaged, and insulted by people who don't know anything about our story or what it's like being trapped in the life every day. But I would go right back out there after every attack because violence was part of the game. At least that's what I kept telling myself to stay sane.

People say horrible things but have no clue that we were once little girls with hopes and dreams taken from us when we were still so young. They have no idea what brought us to this place, the events that caused us to feel like we had no other choice but a life on the streets. We didn't have the choices so many other people have. Once society beats you down, society becomes just as powerful as the pimps. It's easier for society to point fingers and judge than even attempt to help or find out the true story.

Our minds adapt to the environment we are in because of the trauma we face every day; our minds perceive things differently and do seemingly crazy things to protect us. We think love means beatings and violence, that prostitution means power, and that we are worth nothing to most people. The mind is powerful. My mind allowed me to trick myself into believing the worst things so I could survive.

But there were times I was sure I wouldn't make it.

Not in Control

One time I got into a john's car and he had jimmied the door somehow so I couldn't get out. He took me onto the expressway, apparently heading to the location he planned on using to hurt me while he told me everything he was going to do to me. He described horrific things and promised to end it all with murder. I was terrified, but I couldn't get out of that car. If that door hadn't been jammed, I would have jumped out as he sped down the expressway. The farther we got away from the city, the faster he drove and the more sadistic his descriptions became.

I wore thigh-high boots so I could hide a weapon inside the right boot just in case I needed it. I kept it on the right side because that side faced the car door and I could get it out without being seen.

This guy had my face jammed down into the dash, his pistol pressed against my head as he hollered, yelled obscenities, and called me all kinds of horrible names. He kept telling me how he was going to rape me, what he was going to do to me after that, and what he was going to do when he was finished. He described how I would die. I was scared to death, but I knew not to panic. I knew that if I panicked, I would make the wrong move and die. My right hand crept toward my right boot inch by inch.

I whipped out the sharp, slender knife and stuck him in the side, changing his threats to screams. He dropped the gun as he grabbed his side, while I rammed the window with my elbow as the car slowed and started weaving erratically across the expressway. Finally I shattered the window, scattering glass all over me and leaving shards sticking up from the car door. He zigzagged down the highway, bleeding and screaming, as I raised myself through the window and kicked him at the same time. I threw myself out of the window onto the expressway.

I landed hard, my back torn up by the glass left in the window. I crawled into the grass along the road and hid, knowing that if he found me, my life was over. He circled back to look for me, calling me names, and I knew if he found me, I'd be dead.

"Oh, Candy, Candy, Candy," he sing-songed. "I'm going to find you and kill you. Oh, Candy." He searched but never found me in the grass, eventually taking off in his windowless car. I know he was bleeding because I stuck him quick and hard.

I waited a long time on that lonely highway, afraid he'd come back again and find me this time. Eventually I began to make my way back to Grand Rapids, walking along the expressway, crying and bleeding and bruised. I have no idea how long I walked in the dark night, thinking every headlight I saw could be him coming to kill me. I was terrified of him but also scared my pimp was going to beat me for not having the money. Either way, I was in trouble. And so angry with God for letting this happen, for letting my life be so awful.

"Why, God, why?" I cried, still shaking from the encounter. "Why is this happening to me?" I wailed, snot and tears running down my face.

A car pulled over up ahead and stopped; I froze, thinking it was him.

"Do you need a ride, honey?" came the quavering voice from the car ahead of me. "We'll take you where you need to go."

An elderly white couple sat in the car, asking me, a black woman, if I needed help.

"Thank you," I said, grateful and surprised.

They took me to the hospital, not asking questions or lecturing or preaching. I simply got out of the car and they drove away. I'll always remember seeing them waving to me as if I were their best friend as they left the parking lot. Then they were gone, just like that.

I had cuts and abrasions that they treated at the hospital, then I called my pimp and he came and got me. He asked me if I was OK, then, "Where the money at?"

We got back to the house, and he slapped me around because I should have known not to get in the car. I went out again that night because I had to get that money.

A couple years later I was stabbed severely by a john after I got into his car. Again, we were on the expressway. He must have dumped me out of the car because I woke up on the S-Curve, a dangerous section of expressway that weaves through downtown Grand Rapids.

Once again, an elderly white couple stopped to check on me after they saw my foot sticking out onto the busy road. They called an ambulance and waited there with me for it to come. They followed it to the hospital and came into the emergency area behind me.

I didn't know they had come into the hospital. I looked up from the table where they were working on me, blood everywhere, and I saw them. They waved to me, but when I turned my head to look for them again, they were gone.

I was in and out of consciousness as the medical team treated my stab wounds.

"If she hadn't been doing what she was doing, this wouldn't have happened," I heard a nurse say during one of my conscious moments.

I'd have rather died alone on that S-Curve than hear something so hateful from the people who were supposed to help me. They truly didn't understand that there was so much more pain than that of the stab wounds. The wounds hurt, of course, but the pain went much deeper. It was a heartfelt pain that I'd been feeling all my life.

Years later when I got my life together, God brought those elderly couples back into my mind's eye. I realized then that the two couples who had saved me years apart were actually the same people. How could it be that the same couple saved me twice so many years apart? I know the answer. I believe they were angels sent by God to save me. The coincidence was so great that it could only have been God orchestrating my life for his purpose. I thought I had control, but I didn't.

A Friend for Life

There were good things too, bright spots that helped me through. My best friend during those years was Elizabeth Ann Camstra. We met on the corner of Division Avenue and McConnell Street when I was twenty-one or twenty-two; she was a couple of years older. She lived across the street from the Acapulco Restaurant. When we first met, we were both in the life. We didn't like each other at first, but later on we became the best of friends, closer than sisters even, and we thought of each other as sisters. She had a key to my apartment and I had one to hers; I would go to her house to sleep and she to mine.

We partied at the bars together, worked the streets together, went to jail together, even got out of jail together. We'd holler up and down the jail hallways to each other. "I love you," we'd yell back and forth. We never betrayed each other either, even though the police wanted us to turn on each other. One time she was arrested and jailed, her bond set at five thousand dollars. I got that money and paid her bond. She didn't ask me how and I didn't tell her, but I got it. That's the kind of friendship we had, a sisterhood that was unshakable and unbreakable.

Once I got a call that Ann (that's what I called her) was at the Hideaway Bar, about to get into a fight. I hurried down there and stood back-to-back with my best friend, fighting anyone who came our way.

When I had to leave for California with my pimp, Ann begged me not to go. I told her I had to get up out of there because there was a warrant for my arrest. I asked her to come with me, but she didn't. She had a man in Grand Rapids she didn't want to leave. We cried when I left, me telling her to come with me and she telling me to stay.

Even in death, she is still my best friend thirty-some years later. I was alone all my life, but then I found that friend who was a true friend in every sense of the word, who the police couldn't even make betray me. I knew her so well and she knew me so well that we never believed the lies people tried to tell us about the other. We knew they were lying because we had no secrets from each other.

We were separated during the time I spent in California, but she was still in my thoughts. One night I was sleeping when a cloud came through the door, then Ann came through. I was so happy and excited; I kept asking how she got there. She kept saying she loved me, she loved me, she loved me.

"I hear you, Ann. How long are you staying? Let me make you a pallet to sleep on," I said.

She kept saying she loved me and that no matter what, she would always be here with me, then she left my room. I still don't know if I was awake or asleep.

I got a call the next morning that Ann had killed herself.

Ann had come to me the night before, already dead, to tell me she loved me. I felt angry and hurt that she had left me behind. I had never had a friend like her, but she couldn't hold on. I had told her I was coming back, but she couldn't hold on.

To this day, I don't think she killed herself by blowing her brains out. I believe someone else did this to her. There are so many inconsistencies to the story, but the police don't care. She's just another dead ho. But not to me. I won't let her death be in vain. I know that if she were alive, she'd be clean and we'd be doing this life together.

I didn't come back to Michigan for the funeral, and I still haven't visited her grave.

Yet, she still lives. I had gotten my life together and was driving down Eastern Avenue one day when my phone rang.

"Is this Leslie? Do you know Elizabeth Ann Camstra?"

"Who is this?" I asked.

"This is Sherita."

"Sherita, my goddaughter?" I yelled.

Sherita, Elizabeth Ann's daughter, had been looking for me all these years.

When she walked up the stairs at our first meeting, I could have fallen down dead. She looked identical to her mother, though not as tall. I was able to talk with her about her mom, about our love for each other and our deep friendship. Sherita and I still keep in touch, and she keeps asking me to go see her mom's grave. I know I'll go eventually, but I'm still not ready because I'm really angry with her, after all these years, for leaving me. But I know in God's time, he will lead me to her grave.

Moving Around

The Stable didn't stay in one place all the time. Grand Rapids was home, but my pimp traveled "the circuit," hitting big events in a variety of cities. We drove in a sort of caravan—four or five pimps in their big Cadillacs with their girls going from state to state. We were sold ten to fifteen times a day, six days a week. We were grateful for that one day off a week.

There is something about the street life that looks attractive. It's about being in the middle of things, the bars and the parties, the clothes and money and alcohol. It was lights, camera, action all the time. We traveled from city to city, seeing the brightest lights and the hustle and bustle of the underworld. But then we were stuck in hotel rooms that were dirty, sleazy places, servicing men.

Richard Lapchick, a contributing writer to ESPN.com, wrote a column on July 30, 2019, the World Day Against Trafficking in Persons set by the United Nations.[1] He reported, "Large sporting events such as the Super Bowl or NCAA Final Four are prime targets for human traffickers because of the number of people who converge onto a city during these events. The situation frequently revolves around men who are . . . without their partner in an environment where there often is a significant amount of alcohol being consumed."[2]

---

1. "World Day Against Trafficking in Persons: 30 July," United Nations, accessed May 13, 2021, https://www.un.org/en/observances/end-human-trafficking-day.
2. Richard Lapchick, "The State of Human Trafficking and Sport in 2019," ESPN, July 30, 2019, https://www.espn.com/espn/story/_/id/27263771/the-state-human-trafficking-sport-2019.

I know this is true. We traveled to large sporting events for years, taking advantage of the ready market for prostitution. We were part of the sport for the johns, part of the experience of heading to the big city to enjoy a woman and a game. We even traveled to northern Michigan during deer-hunting season, the perfect time for men to indulge their fantasies far from home.

Wherever there was big money and booze, we were there: the Kentucky Derby, Super Bowl, Rose Bowl, Masters Tournament, and World Series, plus many more. We were in every major city. If the end goal was to be in California for the Rose Bowl, we headed out weeks ahead of time and stopped at various cities and small towns along the way to be sold to men who were willing to pay.

For years I traveled with my pimp. But after he went to jail, I traveled on my own.

Through a silent network, I knew which bartenders would accept payment to let me work the bar. The bartenders talked to the men and directed them to me; they also knew which men were the police. A lot of the bars I worked were inside luxurious hotels where I had rented a room. Once the deal was made, the john met me in my room. I wore expensive business attire to fit in with the crowd in those bars; nobody ever knew the difference. I paid the bartender for the business he sent my way.

In all those cities, at all those events, whether I traveled with my pimp or on my own, I knew one thing: I would never, ever not make money because johns are everywhere.

I spent the decade or so of my twenties traveling the circuit or working on South Division. My pimp and I also spent two years in California. I worked, of course, sometimes standing on street corners but most of the time inside hotels at the bar and also at house parties in Hollywood Hills. He oversaw all that work.

Eventually he flew back to Grand Rapids to visit relatives, he said, though I suspect he had some other things going on.

Whatever it was, it got him arrested and locked up in Grand Rapids. About that time, I found out I was pregnant with his child, and I made the choice to keep the child. But I was happy he was locked up. I flew to Grand Rapids and went to visit him in the county jail. One of his other women was visiting at the same time, and she wasn't thrilled I was there. In fact, she threatened to kill me and my child; we got to fighting right there in the visiting room, going at each other with fists and kicks and screaming like crazy.

The guards put a stop to it, telling me that C wanted to see me and not her. I got to visit with him in the jail, where he discovered I was pregnant. That conversation was a turning point for me. I knew, after all the beatings and him selling me, that I was finally free. He was in jail and couldn't control or hurt me anymore. Little did I know, I was walking toward the light.

Trying to Live Free

I flew back to California—in part because I had a round-trip ticket—and delivered my son the day after Christmas. I had been living with my grandfather Jack on West 67th, in a Los Angeles neighborhood known for its gangs. The Crips ruled the streets there and I knew it. Everyone did, and every kid knew he'd become a member of the gang someday. I had gotten a job at a telemarketing firm—which was strange for me, but I was making an effort—while I waited for my baby to be born. I was so happy when he finally came.

As I got out of the car with my newborn, right from the hospital, here came the leaders of the Crips, who lived on my block. They all wore blue rags to mark their gang affiliation. They walked up to me and my baby and put a blue rag on my son.

"Welcome home, young Loc," they said.

Loc was gang language for a Crip. They were already marking my newborn son to become one of them. I knew then I had to get my child out of there. A few months later, I packed up my stuff and came back to Grand Rapids.

I lived temporarily with my mom and my oldest son, whom she was caring for. Soon, however, I got my own apartment on Putnam Street, where I lived with my new baby. I stepped right back into prostitution when I got home because I knew no other way.

I had a number of regulars in Michigan who had kept in contact during my time in California. They called me to talk, and I told them what they wanted to hear. The money would arrive in the mail soon afterward. Once I was back, my regulars started coming around again. They were happy I was in Grand Rapids and eager to get back to our usual transactions. I paid a babysitter to watch my son, then met the men at a hotel of my choosing.

I was in charge now, with no pimp in the picture. I decided when, where, and how much. I was sure I was in control.

Dear Reader,

No woman, no matter what she does to get by, deserves to be hit, stabbed, slapped, threatened, or raped. When you are forced to have sex against your will, it is rape.

Health-care personnel are often on the front line of caring for prostituted women.

Emergency room nurses and doctors care for wounds inflicted by johns or pimps, and are often the health-care providers of choice for dealing with things like STDs, infections, overdoses, or ailments caused by exposure to the elements. Please know there is so much more to prostituted individuals than what you see or think you know. Each one is someone's child; each victim was once a little girl or boy who had hopes and dreams. Please give us respect and dignity. Please understand we'd rather not be where we are and we don't need to hear your judgment.

So many people don't have choices. Their childhood circumstances, the traumas they've experienced, their socioeconomic status, their race and gender can all conspire to eliminate choices others have. Please, please give these individuals a chance. Understand that their "choices" were often no choice at all.

All of you deserve so much more than a life without choices. You are valued by God, you are his creation, and you are loved. Please know that no prostituted individual deserves to be treated like trash. All of us are treasures in God's eyes.

Love, Leslie

Join the Revolt

1. Think through the choices you've made in your life. What were your options? Compare the options you've had with the options that I had. What are the differences?
2. List some of the things your church or ministry could do to offer prostituted individuals more choices in their lives, such as helping with education, job skills, food, or housing. What would it mean for your group to offer these options?
3. Think about how you can give a voice to those who have no voice. Can you help them write their stories? Listen to their stories? Expand this to include the elderly, the lonely, immigrants, single parents, and other marginalized people.
4. Decide how you are going to change the narrative you've created about individuals who have been trafficked. What new narratives regarding lack of choice, fear, and trauma give these individuals dignity and self-esteem instead of shame?

Chapter 5

HITTING THE BOTTOM

When I was first brought to C's house as a fifteen-year-old child, I knew nothing. I didn't know what I was supposed to do. The mental and emotional strain was horrifying. But I learned the game real quick by watching the older women who had been out there for years. I also learned from the many beatings I got. I picked up fast on how I had gotten out of pocket and changed my ways accordingly because I was terrified of C. I was expected to make a quota to give my pimp every day. The quota amount changed throughout the week, but Thursdays, Fridays, and Saturdays had higher quotas. More johns were out on the weekends.

We did whatever we needed to do to reach that quota, including clipping tricks.

Sometimes I clipped money from tricks because I was tired and wanted to stop working for the day. Clipping tricks was also a way to make our pimp happy. Every once in a while we stashed money on our persons where C couldn't find it.

I clipped tricks many times. I was more scared of what my pimp would do if I didn't have the money than of what the tricks might do to me. Most of the time they didn't know I had clipped them until I was gone. Once they figured out what I had done, they came back to the Stroll looking for me. But after I clipped a trick, I went to the house and changed my clothes and hair, my total look, so they wouldn't recognize me. A couple of times, johns came back to the Stroll at a later date and remembered who I was and threatened to call the police. The thing was, what were they going to tell the police? That I had stolen their money when they were buying sex? A couple of them did report the theft, but the police didn't do anything. They asked the johns why they were down there buying sex in the first place.

C took care of us by buying us clothes and food. Of course it was with the money we earned. He bought a lot of clothes from boosters, people who went into stores and stole thousands of dollars' worth of clothes without being detected. He bought clothes from boosters because he didn't want to spend a lot of money on clothing. Buying clothes from boosters was half of the retail price.

I watched other women out on the Stroll with expensive clothes and furs, and I admired them. They were sharp. When they put on those clothes, they seemed to shrug off the cares of our world, and I wanted to be just like them. On a day off, I went to one of the big clothing stores downtown—at the time there were Gantos, Herpolsheimer's, and Steketee's on the Monroe Mall—with one of my wives-in-law. We got to the store and started looking around; I watched her roll up these expensive dresses and put them up under her skirt and into her girdle. She looked around to make sure no one was watching, took the dress off the hanger, rolled it up, and lifted up her dress. Right there in the open. I, too, had to learn how to steal what I needed in order to make money.

A lot of times we were forced to boost clothes to wear out on the Track. It was like a competition to see who could look the sharpest, to see who was the baddest bitch out there. We wanted the good stuff so we took ourselves to the high-end stores to boost expensive dresses and anything else we needed.

All of our obsession with looking good and having expensive things was really about self-esteem, self-worth, and making money. I didn't even know I had issues with self-esteem and self-worth until I left the game and really started working internally on myself, but looking the part helped me to meet my quota on the Stroll.

Life in the Stable

The house where we lived was run by the bottom. The bottom was really the top. She was the woman who made sure all the girls did what they were supposed to do. I was supposed to turn tricks, give her the money, provide sex for my pimp, and worship the ground C walked on. I was a teenager when I got there, but as I got older I learned how to survive in the darkness.

By the time I was in my twenties, I had turned countless tricks and experienced more horrors than anyone could ever imagine. I knew how to survive on the streets, how to make money off tricking, and how to please C. The day went smooth when C was pleased. When C wasn't pleased, we walked on pins and needles, not knowing what to expect. I could sit there having a conversation with him and say something wrong, most of the time not knowing what I said to set him off. All of a sudden I'd get smacked in the face because I was out of pocket.

I looked up one day and the bottom was no longer there. I hadn't seen her for several days and I was too afraid to ask any questions. Everybody wondered where she was, but we knew better than to ask C. You got to roll with the code of the streets, and one of the codes is that you don't ask questions at all. Everybody kept doing their thing in the house like nothing was wrong.

A couple of days after she was gone, we got in the car and C dropped us off on the corner. The next thing you know, he came, picked me up from off the corner, and told me what I was sup-posed to do as far as making sure the girls were out working. If they didn't behave and make their quotas, it fell on me. I would get beat because I was supposed to let him know when they didn't make their quotas or got out of pocket. He ruled with a steel fist and I knew it.

I, who was once on the bottom of the list, became the top. I didn't want the job but was forced into it by C when the other bottom came up missing. I had to make sure that the four other girls were on the corners where they were supposed to be and that they weren't hiding money.

I collected the money and passed it along to C. I knew many of C's moves and moods, but I didn't know every detail. He was out there knocking bitches, preying on unsuspecting women like he had done to me. When he brought them to me, my heart just broke for so many of them. I remembered how I had gotten to this place and knew many had taken the same path and ended up trapped.

These women were all different ages and from all different places. They were on the dark streets alone, sometimes local girls looking to escape a troubled family, many struggling with low self-esteem. Some were runaways who thought life would be better far from home. C would meet them at a bar or bus station, or hanging out in the park. Or he would meet another pimp who would sell a girl to him. Pimping is a predatory business, and C knew what to look for when knocking a bitch.

Leadership Style

Not all bottoms are the same. Some were horrible, cruel, and mean. Some enjoyed beating the other women, especially in front of their pimps. They liked the control they had over people, but that wasn't my style. I was still so young, and the looks in some of the women's eyes bothered me because they had no clue what they were getting themselves into. I didn't want anyone to go through what I went through. Think about the many masks I had worn throughout the years; all my life I had been a protector. So in my role as bottom, I was more of a protector than an enforcer.

There was a lot of death out there on the streets. A trick slit the throat of one of the women in our Stable. As much as it hurt to lose her, as horrible as it was, I had to keep working. I couldn't let my emotions override what I had to do: keep the girls working, and keep myself working and safe. This woman's death was one more thing stuffed down inside me.

Sometimes the girls didn't make their quotas. Candy, my alter ego, would step out and make up their quotas for them so C wouldn't beat them. They were petrified of him and those beatings, and I understood completely what would happen if they didn't have that money. I was protecting them, often at a cost to myself, from the hands of a brutal pimp.

I remember one young white girl who had thick, long red hair and freckles. I was sitting in the bar with C while he and another pimp talked. I had to look down, not look the other pimp in the face. The rule was that if you looked at or socialized with another pimp, you had to break yourself—everything you had went to him. You chose up a new pimp. I didn't want to risk that, so I listened with my head down.

They were talking about this white girl, with C telling the guy how much she was worth and how much he'd paid for her. The other pimp talked about her not making money for him and how tired he was of beating on her. All along, they and I knew the girl was way under age; she looked older than what she was. A couple days later, C came through the door with this girl. He'd bought her.

She came in nervous and scared, and I understood that all too well. Looking at her that day, I knew she wasn't going to make it. I knew it for sure. C talked to me and the others, introducing her as our new wife-in-law, and this poor girl was sitting next to him, not really understanding what was going to happen. She looked real nervous.

That first night she didn't make her quota so he beat her with a belt and a hanger. He made us watch, like he had done on many occasions. That was another fear tactic C used: have us watch him beat other girls. And when I say beat, I mean literally blood gushing from their bodies. But C and other pimps never bruised the face. You very rarely saw a woman out on the Stroll with a bruised face, because the first thing tricks looked at was the face. A messed-up face meant no business. However, if we saw a woman with a bruised-up face, that meant the pimp didn't want her, that she wasn't making money and it wasn't going to be long before she'd end up missing. A lot of women came up missing. That was nothing new on the streets.

After C beat the red-haired girl in front of us, my heart went out to her. I wanted to reach for her, to soothe her, but I couldn't because C would turn his anger on me. I sat there showing no emotion, but deep inside I was torn up. He yelled, "Fix the bitch up so she can get the f--- back to work, and if any of you bitches try that s---, you hos will be next."

He stomped out the door. I went over and got her up, her body bruised real bad. She stared at me with this "please help me" look in her eyes. I was terrified for her and terrified for myself as I began trying to figure out what to do for her and how to do it. I came up with a plan that I put into action several weeks later.

I had been stashing money bit by bit, eventually saving enough to get her on a bus out of Grand Rapids. I told C I was going grocery shopping, which I did, but I stopped at the bus station on the way and bought a one-way ticket. That night after C dropped us off on the corner, I called someone I trusted and knew really well. That person pulled up to the corner where the girl and I were standing (I made sure she was working with me that night). As she was getting into the car, I told her, "If you ever come back to Grand Rapids, I'm going to beat the s--- out of you." I said that to her to put fear into her so she wouldn't return and wind up in the same situation again. That person took her right to the bus station, and I never saw her again.

I saw the pain in these girls' eyes, felt their pain in my heart. Several wanted to get out of the game desperately but had no money or means to get home. I wanted to save these girls and did what I could to help them.

"C," I'd say, all upset and urgent, "Misty got into a dark blue car last night with a trick, and I haven't seen her since. Have you seen her?" Or, "I think Dandy ran away! I can't find her anywhere."

Invariably, C would stomp around, cussing and yelling, and maybe even make a few phone calls. I knew he would never call the police or file a missing persons report because pimps don't do that. Calling the police could get you killed. I counted on this, because I knew exactly where the girls went.

I had given them bus money and taken them to the station.

"If I ever see you in Grand Rapids again, I'll beat the s--- out of you," I told each and every one of them. "You get on this bus and don't ever come back."

I never saw one of them again. And I never told C, who would have killed me on the spot.

Sinking Even Lower

I continued in my role as bottom for several years, watching young girls come and go, watching as women wound up dead weekly, not knowing if it was a john or a pimp who killed them. Then came the time for change. C and I both had warrants out for our arrest, and that's when we headed to California. He sold the five other girls in the Stable to other pimps before we left.

As I said before, I had a child by C during this time, my second son who was born at the end of 1986. He looked just like his father in many ways, but I also see a lot of me in him.

When C wasn't around, I did pills like Valium and yellow jackets, the street name for speed. Thanks to the drugs, I didn't have to think and feel. When I was a child, reading books and living in fairy tales was my escape. As an adult, drugs helped me to escape the reality I was in.

The mental aspects of prostitution were more overwhelming and harder to overcome than the physical aspects. My messed-up brain couldn't get past the feelings of hopelessness, despair, and worthlessness, a perceived lack of options, and miserable self-esteem. I took more pills. And that's when I fell into the deeper hell called cocaine.

In all those years living in California, which was way ahead of West Michigan when it came to available drugs, I never once tried crack cocaine. I didn't want to mess with the drug at all, though I saw it being used on the streets all the time. I saw what it did to people, and I wanted no part of that.

But I got back to Grand Rapids, back into the life once more, and crack cocaine was part of the game. I met up with my cousin one night and we started drinking. I was inebriated and out of my head when she said, "Here, try this s----." I let her talk me into making a horrible decision.

I took my first hit of crack in 1987.

I can't explain how addicting crack cocaine is. One try and I was hooked immediately. I went from sniffing it to smoking it. I just kept smoking it again and again, and my life spiraled downward. I let my cousin's friend's kids watch my son; I didn't care about anything except getting high again.

I was also in and out of jail and institutions, because when you have a crack habit, you do just about anything to get that next fix. I was jailed for everything from prostitution to theft to possession of a controlled substance. Eventually my mother came and got my second son. She got custody of him, too, and raised him with his brother. When I look back, I thank God with all my heart that she did that.

With cocaine I was able to numb out the voices, the pain, the memories, the regrets. Getting high meant feeling good by feeling nothing. I was steadily spiraling deeper and despising God even more. How could he do this to me? Why didn't he love me? God wasn't real anyway. Life was a day-to-day struggle for survival.

The cocaine pulled me further and further into the darkness. Even with C in jail, I continued to sell myself. How could I do something different if I didn't know how? I became a "renegade." A renegade is a prostituted individual who isn't owned by a pimp, who instead works on her own. I was my own boss, so I thought.

When I was high, I forgot about the degrading things I did, but as I came down, I would remember and had to get high again right away so I didn't have to think about or feel anything. I had done a lot of things in my life that were painful to think about, from stealing to prostitution, from not raising my kids to a million other things. Drugs numbed me out, quieted the voices in my head that kept asking, *Why me? Why did all this bad stuff happen to me?*

Cocaine pushes users further into hell. I became a prisoner to the dope, and that was scary because with prostitution I sold my soul to the devil, but I would do anything—and I mean anything—to get drugs. The darkness shows you all these beautiful things, the bright lights and the hustle, but in the end you have to pay, and you pay with your soul and maybe your life.

I was surviving at this point, but not living. I was homeless, sleeping in abandoned houses and buildings, eating out of McDonald's garbage cans after closing because I had heard they threw away food. I was existing at animal level. I would turn tricks and get high, turn tricks and get high again. I was in and out of institutions, in and out of psych wards and rehab centers and jails. Nothing worked.

Satan was on me constantly, telling me all kinds of negative stuff. "Your children hate you. Your family hates you. You are worthless and cannot be anything but a lowlife ho." I was so spiritually dead that I let it all wash over me.

I had two more sons, in 1992 and 1994. I didn't get clean when I was pregnant so they were each born with crack in their tiny bodies. Both of my last two children were caught up in the social services system, so I would go to treatment centers to try to get custody of them. I wasn't understanding how messed up I was on the inside, how the things that happened in my childhood really destroyed me. I was afraid and really didn't know or understand the depths of what all that trauma had done to me.

Back then you were labeled a prostitute or a ho, and with that label came immediate and huge negative connotations. I was afraid to talk to somebody about it because I didn't trust anybody. The people who were supposed to love and care for me didn't, so in my mind, what made others any different?

I didn't know who Leslie was. I knew who Leslie could become at any given time because I wore so many masks. But who could I trust to help pull me out of this grave? Back then, nobody.

I was going through rehabs and doing the best I could. But when you don't work on your core issues, your issues work on you. I would get my babies back, only to lose them again. I hadn't dealt with that little, wounded biracial girl. I didn't know how. I failed every time.

Then again, a lot of people failed me too. And the system failed me. I see now the system is set up for failure anyway. A few really want to help, but for others it's just a job. We are voiceless and faceless people.

I tried to take care of my babies. I truly did, but mentally and

emotionally I couldn't do it. I loved them, but I realized the best
thing I could do for all my children was to give them to someone
who would love and take care of them. I was too damaged psy-
chologically and emotionally, and no way was I going to take my
babies down with me. My youngest sons were eventually adopted
together. As much as it pained me to adopt them out, I knew—with
all the mental, spiritual, and physical decay I was in—I was saving
their lives. If I was going to be out on the streets and die there, I
was going to do it alone. Inside I was already dead, so I figured it
wouldn't be long until the outside caught up.

Holidays and my children's birthdays were the worst. I wanted to
get so high that I would sleep through everything and didn't have
to think or feel anything about my family celebrating together. I
used to drive by my kids' school and sit there crying, watching my
sons play at recess. My boys looked healthy and happy.

I wanted to die because everyone was with their families except
me. I was out there, empty, lost, and constantly alone, walking in
the rain with nowhere to go. Crying, crying, crying. I lived wherever I could, including my car. I made money by turning tricks
and boosting, which of course got me arrested. I had no contact
with my family. They didn't know where I was, but I knew where
they were. I sometimes spotted my little brother and sister on the
streets, and I tried to hide from them, as I didn't want them to see
me that way.

This was the lowest point in my life. I had four babies that I
couldn't care for. I had no friends, no home. The thing I knew best
was the devil.

The world was totally dark; even when the sun came out, it
was dark. Nothing in my life was sunny. I didn't like to be out in
the daytime, so I roamed at night. I was comfortable in the dark
because I knew it well. Sometimes I'd be up for days and days and

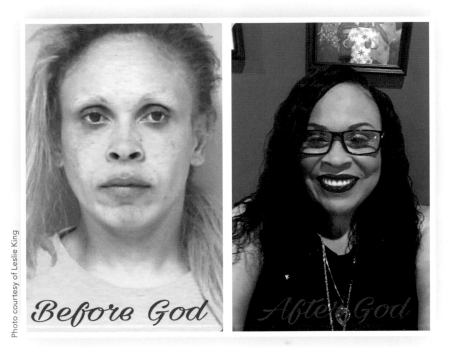

(L) Twenty-something Leslie poses for photo taken by her pimp. Grand Rapids, Michigan. 1984. (R) Leslie, a 15-year survivor of sexual exploitation, at the opening of the first Sacred Beginnings home. Grand Rapids, Michigan. 2005.

Founder and CEO Leslie celebrates the opening of the second Sacred Beginnings home in Grand Rapids, Michigan. 2006.

Leslie praises God in his beautiful creation in Hocking Hills, Ohio. 2017.

Police officers pose for a photo with Leslie after her speech in Flint, Michigan, on sexual exploitation and human trafficking. 2019.

Top: Leslie protests a Grand Rapids, Michigan court trying a 15-year-old victim of sexual exploitation as an adult. 2016.

Bottom: Leslie speaks truth and brings awareness to the causes behind sexual exploitation and human trafficking. Detroit, Michigan. 2016.

Women lean in for comfort and prayer as Leslie does street outreach in various locations around Grand Rapids, Michigan.

Top: Leslie tells her life story and of her transformation by God at Forgotten Man Ministries, a ministry to inmates and officers. Grand Rapids, Michigan. 2013.

Bottom: Leslie stops to listen as the Holy Spirit speaks to her during a presentation. Grand Rapids, Michigan. 2013.

#UNBREAKABLE
STRONGER TOGETHER MINISTRY

CRACKING DOWN ON
HUMAN TRAFFICKING

Top: Leslie protests the incarceration of Cyntoia Brown, a 16-year-old victim of sex trafficking, who was convicted of killing a john she believed was reaching for a gun. Nashville, Tennessee. 2019.

Bottom: Leslie films a commercial funded by The Office of the State of Michigan Attorney General on sexual exploitation and human trafficking. Lansing, Michigan. 2017.

Leslie prepares to receive the Survivor Liberator Award, an award acknowledging prominent abolitionists from across the United States. Toledo, Ohio. 2018.

days, smoking dope. I would get high until I passed out. Then I'd wake up and go at it all over again.

I was so low, I knew I couldn't get any lower. I was living in crack houses with other addicts. After one especially bad binge, I woke up in jail to find a Bible right next to me. I was surprised and wondered how it got there. I'd woken up in jail plenty of times and had never seen a Bible right next to me. When I got out a few days later, I took the Bible with me. Maybe an angel had left it there.

It was like that Bible followed me and talked to me, telling my body to do things. For one thing, I didn't want to get high anymore. This was a strange feeling, of course, because I was always running away. I didn't know it was God knocking on my door, letting me know he was there. I readily agreed, however, when someone I knew approached me on the street and asked if I wanted to get high.

We got high, but I realized I wasn't high at all. No matter how much crack I smoked, I was not getting high. It was bizarre, smoking crack and not getting high off of it.

I knew I had hurt my family immeasurably, especially my mom, my children, and my brother and sister. I had disappointed everyone, including myself. Would they ever forgive me? Could they?

A huge rush of shame and guilt fell over me, so powerful, deep, and overwhelming that I tried to commit suicide. I figured that if I smoked a bunch of crack, took a bunch of pills, and drank a ton of alcohol, I would go into a deep sleep and never wake up. The heartache, guilt, shame, memories, pain from my past, and all the names I was called by society would stop, and I wouldn't hurt anymore.

So that is exactly what I did.

Dear Reader,

Every life is worth saving, including yours. No matter how low you've gone, no matter what you have done, your life is worth everything to God. He loves you no matter what. He forgives everything, and forgets all of it in his love for you.

So many people need second, third, and eighth chances to turn their lives around. I encourage you to be patient with yourself if you're trying to create a new life.

For those working with these individuals, be patient as they work through the issues in their lives. Be loving, yet hold them accountable too as they begin to understand what they must do to change. Assisting them in addressing underlying traumas—abuse, violence, rape—will help these individuals understand how causes and effects have impacted their lives. All of this work plays a part in true and lasting healing.

I want all of you—those who are trapped in the darkness and can't seem to find a way out—to know that you are important to God and to me. Remember, many women in the Bible were prostituted women and the chosen ones of God. You can change. You can create a new life.

Every single person has worth.

Love, Leslie

Join the Revolt

1. Think about the labels you put on people. Even "good" labels such as "the smart one" or "the pretty one" or "the jock" can be damaging to a person. How have you labeled others, or how have you been labeled? List those labels.

2. Consider your own thoughts regarding prostitued individuals. How does the label "prostitute" differ from "a victim of prostitution"? Are you able to see them as real people instead of just prostitutes? How has your thinking changed in this regard as you've read?

3. Research rehab institutions in your area, and read up on each one. What are the options for people who need help, and what are people saying about them? Take a tour if you can.

4. Read up on foster care and adoption to see how you might interact with these options in your life or in the life of your church or ministry.

5. What safety nets are available to help young women (and men) who are alone on the streets? How might you or your ministry find these individuals and help them? Look into ways to come alongside young people aging out of foster care as they begin life on their own. Many have not been taught life or coping skills and are easy prey for pimps.

Chapter 6

FREEDOM

July 4, 2000. The day I got free. The day I woke up liberated from drugs and alcohol. The day I stopped being a victim of prostitution.

I had planned to die that day. I drank enough alcohol to kill me. I smoked enough crack and took enough pills to kill me. I was sliding into sleep as I felt my heart go *ba-boom, ba-boom, ba-boom.* These would be the last memories of life as I knew it. When I died, there would be no more thinking, feeling, or pain. Nothing. I wasn't thinking about heaven or hell because I didn't believe in either one. Hell was on earth. I was living in hell. I just wanted to stop all the pain.

I was almost there, almost asleep as my eyes got heavier. My heart slowed, my eyes fluttered shut. I was about to take my last breath, but I had something to do first.

"If there is a God in heaven, if you are real, please just help me," I screamed out. I sobbed and sobbed with my last energy, snot and tears mingling on my wet cheeks and running down my face and neck.

It's almost impossible to describe what happened inside me at that moment. I felt something, something big, hug me so tightly, so warmly, and so filled with love. I knew I was going to be OK. That hug was the moment I knew there was a God. I knew that God had saved me from death and from a life not worth living. He brought me back to life.

I immediately started throwing up. It seemed like all the pain and misery I had experienced—every hurt and memory—was puking itself out along with the alcohol, pills, and crack. It just kept coming and coming as I cried and cried. Finally I got myself up and stumbled out the door to ask someone if I could use their phone.

"Mom, can you come get me?"

She came immediately, so grateful that I was alive. During this time in West Michigan, a serial killer was on the loose. He'd pick up women on the streets, kill them, and burn or mutilate their bodies. In fact, not long after I got clean and started working at Rose Haven, I stopped to talk and pray with a woman. The next day they found her hog-tied and her body on fire. The killer had eleven victims over the course of five or six years.

My family hadn't heard from me in so long that they thought I'd become one of his victims. My mom told me later that she heard something different in my voice when I called, and that made her come right away to get me. She found me sitting on a curb, waiting for her.

Waking Up to a New Life

My mom took me to her home, where I showered and she fed me. I felt so safe because I was home with my mom. I slept for hours and hours in that safe place. When I woke up, the first thing I did was call Turning Point, a detoxification program through the Salvation Army for those with active addictions. I stayed with my mom for a couple of days before checking myself in. She took me to a bunch of thrift stores to buy me some clothes (I had nothing), then drove me to the facility, located in a former hospital in Grand Rapids. I put myself into Turning Point to fight substance abuse and to learn to live without alcohol and drugs.

I remember the doctor there wanting to put me on a medication to help during withdrawal. They do that a lot when people come into the program filled with all manner of substances. I said no. It didn't matter how much junk I was on or how hard it would be. I needed to do this on my own. I was nervous and afraid, but I did it anyway. Nobody was with me, and nobody could do this for me.

Three days of hell later, the staff at the detox center were telling me I couldn't be there any longer due to insurance issues. I was a complete mess. I looked a fright, like I had peed all over myself. But a nurse named Ethel was all like, "Leslie's not going anywhere." I loved Ethel. The push to get me out because of insurance was Satan trying to shut me out of detox since he knew I'd go right back to the streets.

"Leslie's staying here," Ethel said, and told me not to worry about anything. I'd be OK, she said. I'd been in Turning Point several times and knew Ethel from those visits. She was mean as hell; she didn't put up with anything, not one thing, from the people at the detox center. Addicts tried anything—any lie, any trick, any sneaky way—to get drugs, but she knew all of them. She didn't give addicts an inch. But when she stood up for me, I saw her in a different light. We bonded that day and are still in touch to this day. She became a trusted ally in my life from that point on.

After Ethel stood up for me, I went back to my room and saw the purse I'd brought with me to detox. I wanted to get rid of the purse, so I was taking everything out that I needed to keep before I threw it in the trash, like I was doing with my past life. I was getting rid of it all.

Among all the lipsticks and gum and condoms, I found a business card from Sister Francetta of the Dominican Sisters. I don't know how that card got there. I had never messed with those nuns. They used to come down to South Division to try to pray with us, but I never was having any of that. I despised those women of God and wouldn't even touch them or let them touch me. However that card got in my purse, I saw it as a sign from God.

I called Sister Francetta during my time at Turning Point and asked if they had room for me at Rose Haven, a program for prostituted women run by the Dominican Sisters of the Good Shepherd.

Needless to say, Sister Francetta was surprised to hear from me—surprised but willing to help. She came to Turning Point to assess if I might fit into their program, which required I be free from drugs and alcohol. I was, but she told me they didn't have any openings. Could I find someplace to go until they had one?

"No," I said. "If I go out there, I'll die. When I leave Turning Point, I'm coming straight to Rose Haven."

"How do you know that, Leslie?" she asked.

"I just know," I responded. "If I have to sleep on the floor, I don't care. I'm coming to Rose Haven."

She just looked at me, but I knew I was going to go there.

After the initial detox, I began a longer treatment program at Turning Point that meant I stayed there for thirty days. Three days before I was supposed to leave, Rose Haven called and said they had an opening. *Of course they did*, I thought. God was watching out for me. The nuns came and picked me up at the appointed time. I was as scared and nervous when I left Turning Point as I was when I went in.

I was so afraid when I got to Rose Haven. I was afraid of not getting through the program, afraid of my old life, afraid that I'd go back to the drugs and alcohol, afraid that the darkness would overtake me once again. I had to learn how to live and who Leslie was, because I didn't know. I was good at transforming myself into who I needed to be in any given situation—Little Leslie or Big Leslie or Candy or whoever else. But who was I, really? I had no idea.

On the practical side, I was so used to working in the darkness that I could hardly handle living in the light. I had to see a doctor, and he put me on an antidepressant. I wasn't sure about this, but I started taking the pills. Then I went to church with my mother and heard the pastor say that people who are depressed don't need meds—they need Jesus. I felt like God was speaking to me right then. I came back to Rose Haven and told them I wasn't taking those meds again.

I know antidepressants work very well for many people, and I don't begrudge them that. Simply saying Jesus will heal depression isn't the answer either. He can heal it, but he also uses medications to bring about a better life. In my case at that time, I went off medication and did well. I'm so thankful to God for that, but I am also thankful that medications work well for so many who need them. In fact, I'm now back on antidepressants to help me fight PTSD, anxiety, ADHD, and depression.

Victory in Jesus

My mom brought me a little stereo and a CD of Christian music while I was at Rose Haven because I love music. I constantly listened to "Still I Rise" by Yolanda Adams and "Stomp" by gospel singer Kirk Franklin. I love to dance, so I was jamming to the music like I was at a club. I was singing along as I jumped around my room, lost in my own world, not understanding that the words that came out of my mouth were going into my ears and straight into my heart. The words told me I could have victory over the enemy.

I did have the victory, victory in and through Jesus. The lyrics to "Stomp" became more and more powerful every time I sang and danced, which was pretty often. And then it happened: I caught the Holy Ghost in my Rose Haven room with Kirk Franklin playing loudly in the background. I was crying and weeping and praising Jesus, reveling in the Holy Ghost who filled me. Oh, I remember that day so vividly. It was another turning point in my life. The fullness of the Holy Spirit entered me; I felt the magnitude of his grace and mercy to me personally, saving my life. I knew the fight for my life was on. I began understanding what I needed to defeat the enemy, and I was no longer afraid of what my future looked like.

Along with the music, my mother also brought me a book filled with Bible verses called *Scripture Keys for Kingdom Living* by June Newman Davis. I carried that book with me like I used to carry my crack pipes: clutched close to my heart and well protected. Every time I felt fear, shame, loss, guilt, desperation, or anything that threatened to bring me down, I turned to that book and a verse from Scripture. Those Bible verses brought me back from the edge every time.

I never relapsed, never drank or did drugs again. I was sorely tempted from time to time, but God had saved me from that life, and I loved him. He was my Savior, not cocaine or alcohol. I was slowly getting ready for a new life.

Doing the Work

I knew I never wanted to use again, but I also knew I had to work on the reasons that started me using in the first place. I had to ask myself what was really wrong with me and why I was doing the things I was doing. I had to go back and meet that little girl Leslie, all the way back to my earliest memories. I couldn't do it by myself, but I didn't trust people.

It seemed that everyone I had trusted to love and protect me only hurt me.

When I was in Rose Haven, I had a counselor named Everlina. I gave her hell. I was rude, mean, and nasty to her, uncooperative at best. Even though I was there to heal, I made it hard for everyone. This behavior was automatic, a natural defense. But Everlina never gave up. She kept coming and coming and coming, like a bulldozer. The harder I fought to stay away from her, the harder she fought to break down the walls I had. I met with her once a week at first, then several times a week.

Rose Haven residents attended different groups and went to different Narcotics Anonymous (NA) and Alcoholics Anonymous (AA) meetings. One of the NA meetings was on Division Avenue, close to where I had lived and worked. I had a fit because I didn't want to see Division Avenue or go anywhere near it since I was addicted to the lifestyle, addicted to the game. I didn't want any part of that lifestyle and didn't want to be tempted. My hands got sweaty and my heart started racing; I was hyperventilating and having a panic attack, for sure. I was looking through a window at the action outside, and all I wanted to do was run out there and get back into the life. The Rose Haven people had to come get me from that meeting. In order for me to build some kind of strong foundation, I needed to be out of that environment to really work on me. I couldn't be anywhere near the life.

I went to other NA meetings after that, all far away from Division Avenue. Those meetings helped a lot because I found other people just like me—addicts. Anyone can get addicted and I saw them all, from doctors to housewives, from police officers to just about anyone else. I got a sponsor, attended ladies' meetings and other groups. I made friends. We were people from every walk of life, all addicted in some form or another.

I was also going to medical doctor appointments to take care of my physical health, as well as my mental, emotional, and spiritual well-being, something I didn't do while I was addicted. I went to church with my mom every chance I got.

As much hell as I gave Everlina, she gave me hell right back. I was shocked because I couldn't spin her, run game on her, run anything on her. When I tried hustling her, she wasn't going for that mess at all. She was all like, "Stop your s---, Leslie." In my head, she was no different than all the other people in my life who wanted something from me. I told them what they wanted to hear, and they left me alone. I told her what I thought she wanted to hear, and she said, "Leslie, that's not the truth. When you're ready to tell me the truth, I'll be here. If you just want to come every week and shoot the bull, that's fine. I'll be here."

My great-grandmother always said the eyes are the windows to the soul. I could see in Everlina's eyes that she never looked at me as any less than, worse than, or more of a mess than anyone else. So after a few months, I started opening up to her. Slowly but surely. She was pushing me out of my comfort zone. I didn't want to cry in front of her, because to me crying was a sign of weakness. That's another thing you learn out on the streets—crying in private is OK, but you don't cry in front of anyone.

The day Everlina finally broke through was scary. I was vulnerable and that scared me. I started with my childhood, talking about the violence and how I felt during a lot of that. I talked about being raped and all the other stuff. She listened and let me talk. Everlina spoke too, and that's when the healing started. It all spilled out over the course of time.

Starting to heal was like opening up a wound and bleeding all over the place. The bleeding didn't stop for a while, but then I'd sew up that wound and start into the next one, opening that up to bleed all over. Now, however, I can look back at the other wound and see the scar, but it doesn't hurt anymore. I could talk about that wound without it breaking me.

There were so many wounds I opened that were so painful, I didn't think I'd make it through to the healing. Once I opened them, I'd have nightmares and night terrors, some of them so painful, I was almost paralyzed with fear. But I knew if I didn't deal with those wounds, they were going to deal with me. All my life I'd been running. I was tired of running, and there was nowhere else to run. Either I worked on my wounds and healed, or I'd die. Those were the only choices I had.

I had to fight every step of the way. The devil was trying to pull me back into the pits of hell, but I was going to fight against him with everything I had.

By then I had reunited with two of my children, the two boys my mother was raising. My children loved me, but I'd hurt them so much. They were happy I was clean, but they were afraid I'd leave again. They were leery of anybody I befriended or anyone who befriended me because maybe that person was a drug addict and would take me away again. I didn't understand the hell I'd put my babies through due to my own trauma. I knew I wasn't a mother to them at all, but I had to fight for them. I couldn't allow myself to die and just leave my kids wondering. Today my babies and especially my grandbabies are some of the reasons I keep going.

Getting to Know Myself

I had a lot of learning to do. I had to learn to love myself, and I had to learn and explore everything about Leslie. I had to get to know me.

One of the things that surprised me about me was that deep down inside, I was actually a loving and caring person. I didn't see that part of me out on the street. Out there, I didn't care about anything, and I didn't love anybody except my family and my kids; everyone else was expendable, and I treated them that way. "Get them before they get you" was the way I saw the world. I also learned I was a very funny person. I made people laugh. I didn't always intentionally do so, but I made them laugh.

I had to learn to forgive myself. Forgiving myself was the hardest thing I had to do. I had done so much wrong, I didn't think I could be forgiven for any of it. Forgiving myself took time, but the more time it took, the deeper I dived with help from Everlina and my sponsor and the Bible. I kept *Scripture Keys for Kingdom Living* with me at all times.

I know now that if I had tried to start forgiving myself on my own, it wouldn't have happened because I didn't know how. I couldn't have done it by myself. When I finally did forgive myself, I felt freedom—freedom in the most amazing way. I discovered, too, that when I could forgive myself, I could love myself. That was a new concept.

Getting to know myself was surprising and a whole new thing for me. There were so many things I learned about myself and learned how to do. When I was on the streets, I wore makeup because that was part of being in the game. But now I got to sit down and apply makeup differently. I discovered that I loved makeup and doing hair, I loved decorating, and I loved plant life. I loved growing things and giving them life, then nurturing them. I loved all those things and more.

I also became angry. I was angry because so much of my life had been stolen from me. Who knows what I could have been and done if so much hadn't been taken from me. But God's will is great. I understand now that he allowed me to go through everything I went through in order to go back into the dark and assist others.

I can help others through this process of healing because I've been through it myself. You can't take anybody where you've never been. Going back down through all that hell with others and assisting them with finding out who they are—that's awesome. I couldn't do that if I hadn't walked the same path.

As I was healing, I started grieving. I grieved the only life I knew because I had to bury that life. I was grieving for a lot of women I knew who had been murdered, physically hurt, or were still trapped in the game.

It was very hard and quite painful to deprogram and reprogram myself. Coming out of the game, I had a lot of bad habits. Now there was certain makeup I couldn't wear, certain clothing I could no longer wear, certain places I couldn't go, certain people I had to stay away from, and certain music I couldn't listen to because it put me in the wrong mindset.

Some kinds of clothing took my mind right back to the game, to places and things I tried to forget. In order to change, I had to change everything. I couldn't wear thigh-high boots and certain kinds of stilettos anymore. It took me years before I could even wear high heels again.

I began to understand my triggers. What helped me most was doing the hard work to understand the reasons behind a lot of the things I did, and then working on those issues. That's why it's called a process: you have to work on things bit by bit and piece by piece over time. That's what I did, no matter how painful it was, because I truly wanted to live.

Making Amends

Part of the recovery process with both AA and NA is making amends, the eighth and ninth steps in the programs. I made amends to my family because I'd put them through hell, especially my mother, children, sister, and brother. I would see people I knew, especially women I'd worked with on the street, and try to make amends with them for things such as turning them out into the game. I had to apologize and do my best to help them get out of the game.

I remember a young lady whose pimp dropped her off on a corner with me one night. I taught Carrie, then just fifteen, the game as we worked that corner together. When I got my life together, she was still out there. I saw her when I was doing outreach, and I remembered her. I felt so bad for teaching her the game that I sought her out and told her I was sorry. I also told her, "This started with me, and this is going to have to end with me."

I didn't know what I meant when I said it, but I just knew I would be involved. I continued to do outreach, and I'd check to make sure she was OK. She called me from time to time, and when she did, it was like a knife twisting in my heart. What if the next car she gets in is it, and we don't see her anymore? It's going to be my fault. She called me several times because her daughter wound up in the game, so I reached out to the daughter and started talking to her and mentoring her.

Then Carrie called me and said she was going into a treatment program. She did, and in fact she has celebrated two and a half years clean. She's been through my program at Sacred Beginnings as well. She had a slipup when she got an apartment in the area she used to live in; she went back to the life for a little while, then she got out again. We placed her with someone who went through my program, far from her old haunts. She is now doing wonderful and has her own place here in Grand Rapids. I see her and talk to her all the time. Her life in the game indeed ended with me, and I was so relieved for her. I was also grateful to God for allowing me the chance to help her. I don't know about her daughter at this time, but when she is ready to talk to me about it, I'm here.

A couple of the women who were in the Stable with me have been through my program. We sat down and talked about it, and I made my apologies and they accepted them. But they too had learned how to knock a bitch. I told them they in turn needed to reach out to those women they'd introduced to the game and assist them in exiting the life. A few of them are now out of the life, but some are not; they went right back in.

People often say, "Once a ho, always a ho." That's not true at all. I believe it's easier for people to say something like that than to look seriously at the causes that lead to a life on the streets. They are many, varied, and difficult to face. People like to judge; it's almost like they get a kick out of judging people.

For me, my way out took a long, long time. After the thirty days at Turning Point, I stayed at Rose Haven for a year. I finally found some people I could trust with helping me to find out who I was and to heal. Here I dug very deep, finding my spirituality and relationship with God.

Dear Reader,

The road to recovery and a new life is extremely hard and strewn with roadblocks. Those who walk that road face guilt, fear, shame, addictions, darkness, and judgment. The hardest part is taking the first step. To take that first step, you need to be ready. Are you ready?

Perhaps you are a shelter worker or rehab worker who has seen the same story time and time again. Maybe you've even been played a time or two. I ask you to keep working hard, keep hoping and praying as those with such difficult pasts try to find freedom. Just as Everlina and Ethel stood up for me, I ask you to stand up for those who come into your programs. Fight as hard for their lives as they are fighting for their own.

Perhaps you're not working in a shelter or rehab center. Recovery work is difficult and not for everyone. There is no shame in that. But there is still something you can do. I ask you to pray for those who are on the streets now, those who are in recovery, and those working with them. Make those prayers your top priority. Don't judge; don't condemn; don't ignore them. Pray hard and love.

Love, Leslie

Join the Revolt

1. Begin a prayer group that prays specifically for those who are in drug or alcohol recovery programs. Avoid naming names, instead focusing on strength for the journey.

2. Look into providing space in your church or ministry for Alcoholics Anonymous or Narcotics Anonymous meetings. Research the guidelines for AA and NA meetings, as well as the rules and regulations for your ministry or church to host such events.

3. How might you need to make amends to those you have wronged? Perhaps you need to make amends for your thinking about those who have been prostituted or have addiction problems. How do you need to move from judgment to acceptance?

4. Support a recovery program in your area financially and/ or by meeting physical needs such as building maintenance, food, or clothing. Ask the program about specific needs.

5. Put together a playlist of music that inspires you spiritually to listen to as you walk, exercise, or work. Also gather a number of books that inspire you spiritually to keep by your side, and read them as needed. Read a passage of Scripture a day.

Chapter 7

LIFE RENEWED

I needed a job. Rose Haven gave us twenty-five dollars a week for expenses, but it wasn't enough for me. I needed cigarettes, more clothes, and personal hygiene items. Many of the supplies provided by Rose Haven were donated and didn't usually include things for African American hair. I needed to buy products formulated for my ethnicity. Fortunately, we were allowed to get outside jobs. My job skills, however, were sadly lacking, and the skills I did have didn't translate into get-a-regular-paycheck sort of work.

I scoured the newspaper for openings—back when newspapers had job listings—and saw something called a home health aide. I read the job description and thought it looked like the perfect fit for me.

"I can do that. I've been caring for people my whole life," I said to myself.

Funny how I knew how to take care of others, but I didn't know how to take care of myself.

I took the bus to AngelCare Home Care and filled out an application for a home health aide. Of course I had to admit I had a criminal background—if they only knew the half of it!—which turned out to be a problem. They told me they couldn't hire me because of it.

I was depressed and down when they told me this. I was eager to move ahead in my life and ready to try something new, but my background held me back. Like me, so many others have been incarcerated and/or have a record. Society's rules and laws keep people down, even when they have changed and are moving ahead to a new life.

What was I going to do? I didn't know how to do anything else but care for people. As I walked through the building to leave, I thought of when I visited my dying great-grandmother, Clairbell, whom I had known my whole life and whom I loved and adored. I had thought she was in a coma, but after everyone else left the room and I was putting lotion on her legs and talking to her, she opened her eyes and said, "Hi, baby." I was stunned and told my mom, but she didn't believe me until she walked into the room when it was just her and me. I said, "Grandma, it's just me and mom in here," and she opened her eyes and knew us. I was so glad I could visit her and that she saw me clean and sober. It was especially important to me that Clairbell saw me this way.

My great-grandmother passed several months later. I was in my room at Rose Haven when I felt something brush across my face, like the softest kiss; I looked out the window and saw the brightest star. I'm sure it was her shining brightly to tell me she loved me. On my way to church that morning, I had looked up in the sky and seen a rainbow. I remembered from my childhood the story in Genesis of God putting a rainbow in the sky as a promise. God gave me that rainbow as a promise that my beloved great-grandmother was in heaven and that I would be OK.

Those memories were all signs to me, signs that I was on the right path. But as I walked out of that AngelCare interview, defeated and devastated, I still needed a job.

I knew God had a plan for me, but I so wanted that home health aide job. What else could I do? I cried on my way out, noticing a woman standing near the door as I walked by.

She stopped me and asked if I was OK.

"Who, me?" I asked. "No, I'm not OK."

She asked me what I was doing there, and I ended up telling her everything: my past, my hopes for the future, my job interview, my disappointment. She and I walked back into the office building and sat down at her desk.

"For some reason I need to hire you," she said. "Something is telling me to hire you."

I was dumbfounded and could only stare at her.

She hired me! Turns out this woman I'd spilled my story to was the person who did all the hiring and firing at AngelCare. To me, she was my angel. I started a couple of days later.

A New Line of Work

My first client was Miss Sammie, who lived right by Rose Haven. She had Alzheimer's disease so she didn't know me, but there was something about her I loved. It's like we communicated on our own wavelength. I loved her family too, and they welcomed me into their lives. They let me take her to the doctor's office and allowed me to make decisions regarding her care. I became part of their family, and they trusted me wholeheartedly.

Miss Sammie rarely remembered my name, but she called me Aunt Jemima because I wore headscarves to work. I wore them so my hair wouldn't get in the way as I bathed and fed her. She lived with her daughter and her daughter's husband, with grandchildren in and out as well.

Sometimes she'd get to arguing with people in person or in her head. Occasionally she'd say, "C'mon, Leslie, let's go," so she knew my name at least sometimes. The two of us had a bond, something special between Miss Sammie and me. She loved me wholeheartedly, and I knew it. This was a really good thing in my life at that time because, outside my immediate family, I had finally learned how to bond with someone and really care—something I hadn't been able to do in a very long time. This bonding extended to her family as well. Her love for me and my love for her taught me compassion and empathy.

I had been taking care of Miss Sammie for a couple of years, and had gotten married during that time as well. I was pregnant and excited about it, but when I went to transfer Miss Sammie one day, I felt a pull inside me. I didn't think much about it until thirty or forty minutes later when Miss Sammie started pushing me toward the door. I couldn't understand why she was doing that; I thought it was the dementia. But by the time I made it to the door, I felt a sharp pain and saw blood. I went to the hospital emergency room right away. I started bleeding badly as they put a monitor on me to hear the baby's heartbeat. I listened to the faint beat of my baby's heart as blood gushed out of me. I remember hearing my then-husband yell as he and my mom waited outside the room. They moved me into another room where I delivered a baby boy, my fifth. I was just sixteen weeks pregnant. I was able to hold him for a brief time, touch his tiny body and feel his tiny life. Once again I asked God why he was doing this to me. That sweet boy was my last baby.

I took care of Miss Sammie like I would want someone to take care of me when I got older. I cared for her for maybe five years until, one day, I knew something was wrong when I got to the house. She wasn't her usual self. Her daughter took her to the hospital, where she stayed. Miss Sammie went downhill quickly. I didn't visit her there because I didn't want to see her like that and didn't know how to say goodbye. Her daughter later said to me that Miss Sammie told her to tell me that she loved me before she passed. She died in 2005 at age seventy-four.

I went to the funeral and cried the whole time. She looked so young and at peace as she lay there in the coffin. Miss Sammie's death caused a horrible pain in my heart because we were really close. The pain of losing her messed me up because she was somebody who brought me so much joy. I bathed her, fed her, got her dressed, did her hair, and put a little makeup on her some days. We'd sit at her table and talk about whatever came to her mind. I made her laugh all the time. I tickled her and she tickled me. Her daughter made a DVD of Miss Sammie's life, and I was so surprised that I was in it. I still have a candle with her picture on it all these years later.

Caring for Granny

My other client was Granny. She was one hundred years old when I met her, and she had quite a history. She was among those who started the first Church of God in Christ in Idlewild, Michigan. Idlewild was in central Michigan near Baldwin; it became a resort town for African Americans that thrived from the 1920s to the 1960s. Granny had seen it all, from Jim Crow to the freedom of Idlewild, from the Civil Rights Movement to a new millennium.

She now lived in Grand Rapids, cared for in her home by her children, grandchildren, and me. Granny had dementia and never said a word, sitting hunched over in her wheelchair day after day. I bathed her, fed her, helped her to the bathroom, and got her dressed through my work with AngelCare. She used to call me her "gurl," drawing out the "ur" part.

One day I was feeding Granny when suddenly she grabbed my wrist, looked at me, and said, "You have to forgive them." Her head dropped and she said nothing else.

Chills went down my spine and goose bumps appeared on my arms. I knew exactly what she meant. I had to forgive everybody who'd hurt me. My dad, my cousin, my pimp, my johns, my drug dealers, myself. I had to forgive all the people who still had a hold on me. Anger, hatred, and resentment were like hooks in my back that wouldn't let go. The thing was, I had no idea how to forgive that much hurt. I wanted to beat the hell out of all of them and pray for forgiveness later.

I did the only thing I knew how to do: head back to Rose Haven and try to forgive. I repeated again and again, "I got to forgive them. I got to forgive them."

My forgiveness prayers got deeper and deeper, and I began to understand what forgiveness was and that I truly *had* to forgive them. I remembered the many Bible verses I had read about forgiveness and the teachings I had read and heard. I knew I had to forgive to set myself free. I don't know how long I silently prayed to forgive all those people, but it was several days at least that I prayed almost nonstop. The prayers slowed, but I could feel myself getting free. It wasn't easy, but I forgave those who hurt me, and I'm no longer a slave to that awful burden.

I also realized during that time that the things that happened to me weren't my fault. It felt like a black cloud was gone from over me when I came to that realization. I had always blamed myself for what happened to me. It took time to work through my guilt and shame, but that time of forgiveness was a road to my healing.

My beloved Granny died several years later at age 103.

Full Circle

When I stayed at Rose Haven, I used that time to work and save money, as well as heal physically, emotionally, and spiritually. That haven became the place I started meeting the little girl Leslie. I went so deep to find her; I had to go back into my past, and I was starting to remember and feel again.

There were also people I began to trust with the real me. I worked so hard on myself during that time. It was so hard to remember and have to feel all those feelings that came back like a flood that would overwhelm me. But through it all I knew I would be OK.

I kept listening to gospel music (that old Southern gospel), praying, and reading *Scripture Keys for Kingdom Living*, the book of Bible verses my mom had given me. I had people around me too. I had met a couple of people I trusted through NA, so I could go to them if I was overwhelmed. When I was done with drugs, I was done, but it is a daily fight. Addicts aren't cured until the day they die; the reality for me was that I didn't want to die. I knew if I went back on the streets, I would die. But I couldn't live at Rose Haven forever. I eventually got an apartment and started living on my own. I did everything I could to stay strong.

I graduated from the Rose Haven program thanks to Everlina and through the NA program, where I talked to other addicts who had been through what I had been through. Soon after, I became the first resident to ever become a staff member. I was hired as a resident aide, and as such I helped women just like me.

My gift for caring for others came full circle as I began assisting women in recovery who were just like me. I mentored them, loved them, let them yell and cry, and took them to meetings. I also assisted them with their sexual exploitation issues, becoming a listening ear and helping them face and deal with the trauma and horror of the years they were victims of prostitution.

One time I came in to work and my cousin was sitting there. I was so happy to see her! We laughed and hugged, talked and cried. She was in the program at Rose Haven and began to heal. Her healing started with herself. I was there to listen to these women, just as I had wanted someone to listen to me.

At that time, I worked at both Rose Haven and AngelCare, loving on the scarred women and the beautiful older women who couldn't care for themselves anymore.

Strange Phone Call

Three years later, after much healing and forgiving and living in my own apartment, I started receiving cards from the Grand Rapids Police Department—one from Lt. Ralph Mason, who wanted to speak with me. The police wanted to talk to me? I sure didn't want to talk to Lt. Mason, thinking he had a warrant for my arrest for a crime I'd committed while in the life. I had given the Grand Rapids police a run for their money over those twenty years, I swear I did. I have a collage on my phone of many of my mug shots taken when I was arrested during that time. They are not pretty.

I didn't want to call Lt. Mason back, but I had been reading the devotional *Our Daily Bread* and Bible-based pamphlets. All of them seemed to talk about faith, faith, faith. "OK, Jesus," I said, laughing, "you go see what they want and then come back and tell me. I'm not going to do it." I stalled and delayed and procrastinated about calling Lt. Mason, but I finally did.

You could have knocked me over with a feather. They offered me a job! I was hired by the Grand Rapids Police Department, my old archnemesis, to work with SWAPP (Social Work and Police Partnership) as the outreach coordinator. Chief Harry Dolan started SWAPP in the early 2000s, and I worked with the program all the years it was in existence. It ended when funding was cut. I started out part-time and moved to full-time for about five years.

They wanted me to ride with the police and connect with women on the streets, acting as a liaison between the women, the police, and the social workers. I was to advocate for women in the legal and social services arenas as well as other areas where they might need services.

Wherever they needed help, that's where I was.

I was mentoring and trying to help the same women I used to get high with and stand on the corners with. A lot of us even had the same pimp. But now, instead of getting high with them, I was alongside to help them get out of the life. I had an office in the main GRPD building. I laughed every time I walked in the door.

When they told me I had to ride in a police car as part of my job, I had a fit.

"I'm not getting in that car with you," I would say to the officer.

"It's going to be OK, Leslie," the officer said, laughing at my response.

"No, it isn't," I said right back. "Y'all going to put me in the front seat, and there's a gun up there?"

I was tripping out, but I finally got it together. After so many times riding in the back of a police car on my way to jail, here I was riding in the front seat, hoping to connect with women and help them in any way I could. Here was a new way to care for people, this time from the front of a police car.

I discovered that the police were trained in a particular way, while we women were programmed to deal with police in very different ways. Our worlds collided time and time again. I had some bad interactions with police officers when I was working the streets, but I also had some good interactions. My job now was to bring these two warring factions together, to educate the officers to help the women in the best way possible.

I remember after getting clean that I went to the police department and thanked two male officers who had tried to help me get out of the life. They'd never made me feel less than human and always had empowering words for me. They'd encouraged me numerous times over the years, and I never forgot their kindness.

It felt wonderful to care for women I knew and those I didn't know, using my experiences as a prostituted woman who had been sexually exploited at a very young age, as many of them had been. I was eager to help others get free from that slavery.

Helping women find the resources they needed made me feel like I was taking everything bad that had happened in my life and flipping it, taking the pain from the past and using it for good. I was able to help a lot of women get off the streets, at least temporarily.

Some turned their lives around, but many went back to the life. Some women died, and some are still out there on the streets.

When I saw a woman go back, I understood it all too well because she was me. I'd had chances to get off the streets, to get clean, but I always went back. Changing over to a new way of life is scary when the life you've lived is all you know. Many of them just weren't ready, but I wanted them to know that whenever they got ready, I was right here. I was not going anywhere, no matter what. I met them right where they were.

I also taught the police how to have compassion toward these women, helping the officers understand that this was not a life we just chose one day. I helped them see the women as someone's daughter, sister, aunt, or mother—as a person. I helped them learn not to objectify them or call them names. Each woman is somebody special. Yet I met a lot of officers who were not on board with the chief's plan. They'd ask, "Why do you have a whore working in here?" I couldn't change everybody's thinking, but I had to try, and I helped change some minds.

One thing I didn't like about the police department was that when women got caught for prostitution or with drugs or drug paraphernalia, the police tried to use them in sting operations. They told the women that if they went out and bought drugs from someone, they wouldn't end up in jail. Here I was trying to help these women get off drugs, but the police needed a drug bust so they had these women buy drugs. I confronted a police officer about this one time.

"Well, it's her decision," he said.

"She doesn't know how to make healthy decisions," I fired right back. "If she did, she wouldn't be doing these things. If something happens to her, I'm going to get on the news and name your name and tell them exactly what happened to her. I'm going to hold you responsible."

My words didn't change anything.

We're voiceless and faceless to so many people out there. We're getting used by pimps and johns and our families, and we're getting used by society too. It's no wonder we have trust issues. We're getting used by some of the same people who are sworn to protect us. Forcing us into situations that hurt us isn't any protection at all. There are police officers who still do this kind of thing to this day. Rather than offering women a chance to get off the streets, these police officers throw them right back out there into the darkness.

I met a lot of officers with a whole lot of ego who wouldn't listen to me or go out of their way to help. But knowing them helped me understand that nobody's perfect. Police officers had unaddressed issues too, and I felt sorry for them. I could just imagine how miserable their homelives were. They were trapped inside their own selves. They didn't know how trapped they were, and that was sad for me.

Loving the Job

I loved my job with SWAPP. I knew the street life well, understood the women's trauma well, and understood why they were out there doing what they were doing. At the same time, I was learning more about myself; I loved being a voice for the voiceless, for women who had been exploited one way or another their whole lives.

I truly thought I was going to die on the streets before I got clean. To live this new life was something I'd never envisioned. I didn't have a clue what hope was, so I couldn't miss something I'd never had or do something I had never seen modeled. Everything had always been so negative in my life, so I decided to make every day count by living for myself.

While I had a few police officers who only cared about making the bust and moving up the ranks, there were a few officers who truly cared.

I remember one of the officers they had me ride with. There was a time when we didn't like each other at all. Yet we struck up a conversation because we were riding along together in the car, looking at each other all stupid-like.

I wasn't going to talk to him because I was pissed because he was one of those cops who used to say horrible things about me. But we started talking about my life and the reason I was doing what I was doing. Before I knew it, I just let it all go. I happened to look over at him as I talked and saw that he was crying. It tripped me out because I wouldn't have believed in a million years that a police officer would have empathy for me or a woman like me. He apologized to me, and I was thrown back by that, at a loss for words, but I truly appreciated it. It changed my relationship with him, though I was still leery of the police.

During my time with SWAPP, I was out on the streets with hope instead of despair. I wanted the women to know that if I could do it, they could too. I wanted to be the living proof that we can conquer, and that we can defeat our demons.

I discovered I wanted more. I wanted to do more, become more. If you had told me twenty years before then that I would be helping the GRPD help women like me, I would have thought you were crazy. I would have said I'd be working with those women side by side, still in the game and making money on the streets. But God had something different in mind for my life.

SWAPP was the best thing that ever happened in Grand Rapids, but it was ended before its time. It shed so much light on trafficking and exploitation, but was discontinued because of lack of funding.

LT. RALPH MASON'S STORY

I officially met Leslie in 1986 when I transferred into the vice unit with the Grand Rapids Police Department. She had known me when I was a patrol officer, but I ran into her more often in vice because stopping prostitution was one of our jobs.

She'd be out there hooking, soliciting men, and we'd come around and cuff her up. Back then, Leslie was wild and loud and boisterous; she always wanted to showboat, especially when she was high. But I had a place in my heart for working girls. My grandmother worked in a brothel cleaning rooms, so I always wanted to give the girls respect.

When I was in vice, I came up with a project called FEDUP—Focused Enforcement Directed at Uprooting Prostitution. We were always arresting the girls and not the johns because it was a lot more work to arrest the johns. The theory was that if we took the hookers off the corners, the johns would stop picking them up. But we decided to do something different.

We first watched all the johns' cars and were able to get IDs on them, then we created what we called "delayed cases." We did the same for the working girls, all with the knowledge of the district court. We then mailed letters to the johns, telling them to beware. The media followed me to the post office to record me putting pink envelopes in the mailbox to the johns we had identified.

We had teams go pick up the working girls with delayed-case warrants and had the media following along. I wanted to pick up Leslie because I knew she was going to "perform" for the cameras. Oh my goodness, did she perform for the media. She yelled, screamed, and hollered, but I knew she wouldn't fight me. And she didn't. As crazy as it sounds, we always communicated well.

Years later, GRPD Chief Harry Dolan came up with SWAPP, a program funded by a state grant to help prostituted and trafficked women. I worked with SWAPP for a while before I realized we needed a Leslie, somebody who could communicate with the girls in a way that only someone who's been there could. We knew Leslie had cleaned herself up, and all the cops knew her. But trust is hard for cops. They had locked her up; she had yelled and fussed at them. The issue was whether we could allow Leslie in the building unsupervised.

At first I had to be with her when she was in the building, but eventually she could come into the building alone and at all hours and use the computers. We even attended a conference in Traverse City centered on trafficking, with Leslie and I doing a breakout session together about SWAPP. We talked about our relationship—how I locked her up and fussed at her, and how she fussed at me—and she talked about her journey. There wasn't a dry eye in the place when she got through, and these were a bunch of cops!

"You should have been the keynote speaker," someone yelled.

"Did you hear that?" I asked her.

"What's a keynote speaker?" she replied.

"Leslie, you could have been the main speaker, you were that good," I said.

Leslie is just as tough as you can imagine, but there's been an amazing change in her, a change I've seen with my own eyes. The amount of dedication she has to remaining clean and to helping people is inspiring. She even inspires the officers. One time we were assigned two community service officers who were more interested in going to armed robberies and other "fun" stuff. Leslie convinced them to take one of the girls shopping because she had a job interview and needed clothes. I couldn't believe they did this for Leslie.

She had built trust with them, and once police officers knew she was serious, they'd do anything for her.

Leslie has done so much good; she's helped a lot of women get off the streets. And she has the same dedication now that she had twenty years ago. I know she's saving people's lives, and I'm glad she's still going strong.[3]

Dear Reader,

I want to talk to police officers first. I urge you to remember that the men or women you arrest for prostitution could be your son or daughter. No one is immune to becoming trapped in the game. I don't care if you live in a gated community or the inner city; nobody is immune.

Therefore, treat these men and women as if they were your own child.

Remember that somebody somewhere is grieving that his or her child is out there being exploited, while others don't even know that their child is being exploited. Somewhere out there are mothers, fathers, siblings, children, and relatives who can't sleep for the worry. Every time the phone rings or they see a news story about a prostituted person found dead, they are praying it isn't their loved one.

For those of you living in bondage, know that God has a plan for your life and that he's going to accomplish that plan. Your job is to be open to his leading in your life, to listen to his voice, and to take the steps down the path he puts in front of you. It will be hard,

---

3.   Lt. Ralph Mason retired from GRPD a decade ago, returning to work as a civilian to help with CLEAR (Coalition, Leadership, Education, Advice, Rehabilitation), a prison reentry program designed to reduce recidivism.

sometimes crushingly difficult, but know that God loves you and has your best life in his heart and hands.

For those working with victims of prostitution, your training may be very different from what prostituted women were taught. They are coming from a place of trauma, violence, addiction, and fear and likely won't understand what you're doing or trying to do. Listen and learn as you work with women and men who have been prostituted and traumatized.

People can change. They may need lots of chances, and they will need to be ready, but know that God can work miracles in anyone's life. He did so for me, and he can do so for you or those you work with or love.

Love, Leslie

Join the Revolt

1. Look into programs like Rose Haven in your area and see how you might assist them, including monetary donations and donations of supplies. Ask about the people they serve and gather donations appropriate for that demographic.

2. Think about how your church or ministry helps the older population. How are you ministering to those with dementia and health needs, or those caring for the elderly? Find ways you can come alongside those in your community who need extra help, including partnering with organizations such as Area Agencies on Aging.

3. Consider your interactions with law enforcement. Have they been positive or negative? If you are in law enforcement, list ways that you may have developed prejudices against certain kinds of people. If you are a civilian, add law enforcement and first responders to your prayer list.

4. Think about some of the changes you've made in your life and how hard it was to make them. These changes could be things like stopping smoking, finding a new job, going back to school, or losing weight. What changes do you want to make or still need to make? How is your past impacting those decisions and changes?

5. Think about the following questions. To whom do you need to make amends for making judgments based on inadequate information or your own prejudices? About whom do you need to change your thinking based on new information and better understanding? How has this book revealed your own biased thinking?

Chapter 8

MOVING FORWARD

I dropped out of school at age fifteen and never once thought about going back until I was working with the Grand Rapids Police Department. I didn't make a clear decision to drop out of school, but instead I was constantly running away and then got caught up in the game. My mother would never have let me drop out had she had any say in the matter.

Once I was working for the GRPD, I decided it was time to get my GED (General Educational Development) certificate from the State of Michigan. I headed to the Grand Rapids Public Schools adult education office to see what my next steps might be. Would I need to take a practice test? Sign up for a class? Sit down and take the tests right then?

"You already have your GED, Miss King," the administrator said.

"No, I don't," I said.

"Yes, you do. It's right here in our records," was the response.

So I called my mother after I went home because I knew they were lying.

"Oh, you mean this manila envelope from the state that's been sitting here eight or ten years?" she asked without even hesitating.

Turns out I had taken the GED tests during one of my stints in jail and didn't even know it. I had passed with flying colors.

Having my GED was an important step as I moved forward with my life. I had always been good in school, and I was now on a path that seemed to point to getting a college degree. I started by attended Grand Rapids Community College to get a lot of my basic classes. I was scared. Going back to school after all those years of being in the game was mind-boggling.

When I was in middle and high school, my math classes were all simply "add, subtract, multiply, divide." Then I got into a community college math class, and they were putting letters with numbers and telling me to solve problems. I was like, "What in the world?" I was good at math, but that there? Uh-uh. I couldn't grasp the concept of algebra, but I ended up passing the class thanks to a tutor and studying on my own. I figured somebody had nothing better to do than come up with stuff like that.

I took criminal justice classes and English classes, among the other requirements. I did well and ended up with my associate's degree in two years. I did what I had to do and left, without making any friends. I then transferred to Grand Valley State University to start my undergraduate degree in social work. I started right out taking social work classes, some at the Allendale campus, a thirty-minute drive away, and some in downtown Grand Rapids.

While I was eager to get my degree, attending classes activated my PTSD. I was frustrated with the way the professors portrayed prostitution and drug abuse; to me it was a lot of misinformation about prostituted individuals, and they were being objectified once again. I sat in class just like any other student—OK, maybe a bit older than most!—seemingly absorbing the material. I didn't talk about my life until I started hearing all this misinformation. I was afraid others would judge me; I was in a whole new realm, sitting in classrooms with lots of young, idealistic students who wanted to change the world but had never lived in it.

Also, I was in school with a primarily Caucasian student body.

There were maybe two African American students per class, and mostly they never said a word. I remember sitting in a social work class and this white girl said, "If we assist and help everybody and get them better, we'll be out of a job." I was livid. I told her she was in the wrong field and asked why she was getting into social work in the first place: Was it to assist others or assist herself? We get into social work because we either want to help others or need help ourselves. She definitely needed help.

Another girl was talking before class to the girl next to her and said, "My sister was on Facebook talking with her friends and was talking all ghetto."

"What language is that? What is ghetto language?" I asked her.

She was dumbfounded and sat there with her mouth open. I wanted to know, and I kept coming at her. She got red in the face and said, "I'm so sorry. I'm so sorry." I never talked to her again.

Another girl said she couldn't work "down in that area, down in the hood." I got so frustrated with these kids not knowing or understanding anything. But it made me get vocal with my story and life experiences. By the time I got done with those social work classes, they started to hear what I had to say. They began to realize that the lens they were looking through was blurred and did not give them accurate information.

There was one moment in particular that made me speak up. One of my professors was talking about prostitution and the women who engage in it as if we made a conscious choice to be used and abused by men and had ten other career options to choose from. She was making assumptions and judgments based on what? Her extensive knowledge of what being prostituted means? She was listing on the whiteboard what her research had shown regarding prostituted individuals.

"That's a d--- lie," I said, a little loudly. I was overwhelmed with anger and disappointment because her "knowledge" was so inaccurate about victims of sexual exploitation. She was accusatory instead of being understanding and empathetic.

She turned to look at me, as did the entire class of white students. Once again, I was the little biracial girl who didn't belong. I was too angry to be terrified, thinking of all the women, men, and children I knew who had been victimized, including myself.

"Leslie, I've been researching this topic for five years, and I have a master's degree," she said with a condescending tone.

"You don't know anything. I know because I've lived it for over twenty years," I said, almost crying. I got up and marched out of the classroom with a few students following me, I think because they truly wanted to understand. I could only remember the horror and pain and degradation of being victimized, and I knew I couldn't keep quiet.

I walked right to another professor's office. He was someone I knew and trusted and was a member of the department's prostitution roundtable at that time.

"People are dying," I said to him. "People are dying because no one takes the time to get to know these women. Teachers like the one I just left are labeling them as prostitutes before they even walk in the door. No one is helping if they are labeling these women and aren't studying the causes and effects that lead individuals to get involved in life on the streets. Students are getting wrong information, and it has to stop. People see the effects, but people don't want to take the time to see the causes."

Well, that caused a ruckus. But I would not sit there in silence while people who didn't know a thing about life on the streets expounded on what they thought they knew and solutions they thought they had. They really had no clue.

I didn't go back to that class, but the teacher emailed me a couple of years later to ask if I would come speak in her class. At first I said absolutely not, but after thinking about how I could be part of educating people about the realities of prostitution, I decided to go. The teacher confessed that she herself was ashamed by what she had said to me and her assumptions about individuals who are prostituted. She apologized, and I accepted that apology. I continue to speak to classes at various universities on the realities of prostitution; prostituted women, men, and children; and substance abuse. I continue to have a relationship with that teacher and consider her an ally in the fight on trafficking.

I'm also still in contact with some of those students. They'll contact me if they think a client is being trafficked, and they'll ask my advice. Some of them went into the corrections field, some into social work. A lot of them changed their hearts and minds, and I think I helped them look at their reasons for going into this field. A lot of them learned empathy too. So many of them lived in a protective bubble; they wanted to help people, but the reality of what they were getting into was completely different from what they imagined or saw on TV.

Hot Sauce and Houses

While attending classes and working full-time at the police department as the outreach coordinator for SWAPP, hot sauce seemed like a great idea at midnight one night.

I had no idea that hot sauce would change my life.

I was in the aisle at Meijer, studying my hot sauce options, when I saw a woman I recognized. Darlene had known me since childhood, but I hadn't seen her in years. We talked a long time about what we had been doing, how I was out of the life now and starting over, and how I dreamed of buying a house. Turns out Darlene was a Realtor, and she was as excited as I was about my new life and wanted to help.

That very night, as late as it was, she called someone she knew in the finance business and got me approved for a loan. This was a miracle to me. I could buy a house? I couldn't believe it. I forgot to buy the hot sauce because I was so excited about the possibility of buying a house.

I found the house I wanted, but there were still big hurdles, including that I didn't have five thousand dollars for fees and closing costs. As Darlene and I talked about it, I told her to call the sellers and see if they would either waive those fees or pay them themselves. I don't know where that idea came from because I don't know anything about real estate. She was doubtful because she'd never seen that happen before, but I was confident. If God wanted me to have this house, I'd have it, I figured.

An hour and ten minutes later, Darlene called me, screaming. "They agreed! They'll pay! You have a house!"

It was surreal that I'd have a house, something I could call my own. Something I worked for and hadn't had to sell my body for, and that no one could take away from me.

Soon I was living in my house on Elliott Street, not far from South Division where I was sold and exploited. I loved my house. I spent a lot of time decorating it and making it my own between the hours I spent working with the police department to mentor prostituted individuals and taking college classes.

I was also healing emotionally during this time. I would sit in my home and process the many things that had happened in my life, sort of a mindfulness meditation. One time, while I thought about various events and people who had hurt me, something in particular came to mind. At the reception when my mom married her second husband, I had wanted a piece of cake. My mom said to me as I reached for the cake that I needed to wait because eating like that was why I was so fat. I carried that shame with me through all those years.

Just as I finished that thought, the phone rang. It was my mom.

"Leslie, God just dropped this on my heart. Remember that time about that cake?"

"Yeah, Mom, I do," I said.

"I need to tell you I'm sorry," she said.

Her words took my breath away. Her call was clearly prompted by God. She went on to say that she was sorry for a lot of things in my childhood she didn't do that she should have. She talked about her own childhood and how it affected her. I learned a lot about her that day.

"Mom, I love you so much. You're the strongest woman I've ever known, and you are the wind beneath my wings," I told her.

Throughout all of this, my mom has been able to heal as well. My sister and brother were able to heal too, and we are strongly bonded. To this day, we tell each other "I love you" and hug a lot. Though I didn't get it as a child, I'm now getting as an adult the healthy love and affirmation I craved. I am now a healthy and loving mother to my children and grandchildren.

Connecting with Women

At this time I was connecting with women on the street in new ways as I talked to them about how much God loved them, how I came out of the life, and people and resources that could help. Movement never happened the first time I talked with a woman. I talked time and time again with them, sitting in restaurants, in jail, or along the street, inviting them into my warm car for conversation and coffee, calling them and telling them to call me anytime they needed a friend. Sometimes I helped them get out of jail, went to court with them, or helped them get the health care they needed.

This was all part of my job with SWAPP, but I had already been mentoring women since 2002, about a year after I got clean. People would see me and come up to me, and the next thing you know I'm talking to them about how I got clean and stayed out of the life. Helping just came natural to me because I knew what was going on in their heads, their emotional struggles with trauma, and their physical struggles with addiction. I was running mentoring programs at the jail as well, helping incarcerated women with self-awareness and linking them with services.

Usually it took months or years for a woman to make the decision to get out of the life. Sometimes they never did, too terrified to leave or too unsure of what a new future could look like outside of the game. Occasionally it came down to a panicked phone call late at night and a fast drive to find her and get her out. If a woman called in distress—she just got beat up by a pimp or a john, she was suicidal, or there was some other reason—all I knew was that I needed to get there and she needed me. I dropped everything, especially if it was an emergency. I would find those women anywhere, maybe at a house or a hotel or hiding somewhere until I arrived.

I was threatened a couple of times by pimps, but I wasn't scared of them. I knew the code of the streets real well, so I always rode by the code when I helped women get out.

A lot of women called just to hear my voice. They weren't ready to leave or were too afraid, but they wanted to talk to someone who had been there and could talk to them without judgment. They knew they could call anytime just to say hi and to hear my voice. I received calls all year long, but always more around Thanksgiving and Christmas.

There was one phone call that changed my life. I had been mentoring women for some time, but this was my first call from a woman asking for help getting out.

"Leslie, can you come get me? I'm going to kill myself; I can't take it anymore. Please come get me," the woman cried. I had been working with her over the previous couple of months, help-ing her to think about a new way of living. She finally had had enough. But where would I take her? Was there space at a local shelter? A place for women only? The only thing I knew to do was pray.

"Lord, where am I going to take her?"

The answer was clear: *Right here.*

"Right here? My house?"

I heard Jesus say, *This ain't your house.*

I didn't understand then, but I knew I needed to just go and get her. I went and got her in the middle of the night and brought her to my house on Elliott Street. I picked her up off a corner on the track, on South Division. When we got home, she fell into my arms and bawled and bawled. We talked for hours until she began to settle down. I let her take a shower and fed her, and she went to sleep. She slept for a couple days. When she woke up, we got her into a detox program.

During detox, I made sure she had clothing and personal items of her own. When she went into a long-term treatment program, I came to visit her on family nights, and she would call me to talk. I wanted to make sure she had everything she needed to transition to a new way of life. After long-term treatment, she came to live in my house. She stayed clean for a while, then went back to the life. I still see her every so often.

She was the first woman that I took in, and soon after, I began bringing more women into my home. Sometimes they'd stay for a couple of days, sometimes a couple of months. I was mentoring them, many were detoxing, I was advocating for them, and I was also working with SWAPP. These parts of my life overlapped, but add to the mix that I was in college as well. It was a lot!

Before too long I ran out of space in my house to offer a bed to all the women who needed one. After praying and thinking through the options, I rented another house with money left over from college. With women living in both houses and me mentoring them and advocating for them in all arenas, I didn't sleep much.

This was a time of trial and error as I learned how to navigate caring for these women.

Many who came to my houses were running from the law. I advocated for them to prevent them from spending time in jail and tried to get them into detox and/or other treatment programs. I didn't know what I was doing, just that I needed to do it. I didn't know all the details of how to work in this arena, but I operated off of what I'd experienced when I was in those situations and what would have worked for me.

The same things don't work for everybody, I learned, so I had to meet each woman where she was, whatever that looked like. Everybody operates differently, and each individual is unique. A lot of what I did was intuitive on my part. I lived the street life for a long time so I became very in tune with the way people moved, how they made eye contact, their body language. A lot of the things the women did I had done as well, so I knew what to look for.

I could tell when they were lying to me because they were telling the same lies I had told. I could tell when they were trying to run game on me because I had run the same game. Eventually they came to respect me because I knew what I was talking about.

I was also helping men and transgender people who had experienced the same sort of traumas as the women and had the same things happen to them. I never turned anyone away because problems happen to everybody and everyone deserves a chance.

Throughout this time I was meeting all kinds of people in the community, which was hard for me at first. Some people remembered me and looked at me based on what I had been in the past. This angered me, but then again it gave me a lot of determination to prove them wrong. Some of those I connected with had known me my whole life, and some were new acquaintances. I met social workers, lawyers, and judges, some who were bad and some who really cared. Some gave me the side-eye and doubted whether I was going to make it. I had a lot of people who thought I couldn't stay clean, get a degree, or run a business. But I proved them wrong.

Once I started working on myself, I absolutely ignored what other people thought, and I continued to do my thing—mentoring and assisting prostituted individuals. My life was crazy busy, but I was happy and fulfilled.

While I was learning more and more about how to help the people who came to me and lived in my houses, I was speaking with people in the business world who told me about the non-profit sector. I wondered if I could turn my transitional houses into an official nonprofit. After much thought and prayer, I decided to do so.

Sacred Beginnings Women's Transitional Program is a safe haven that offers hope and healing for those stuck in the vicious cycle of sexual exploitation. I named it Sacred Beginnings because on July 4, 2000, when I tried to commit suicide, God saved my life. It was a sacred experience, that conversation with God, and a new beginning. Every day anyone wakes up is a new beginning. Every time someone escapes the victimization of prostitution, she experiences a new beginning. I love helping others get free from bondage, and I like to think Sacred Beginnings has filled some of the gap left by the demise of SWAPP.

Dear Reader,

The journey to freedom begins with one small step. But those who are trapped in addictions and/or prostitution have to be ready to take that step, to move from victimization to victory. There are organizations and people who will help, but each person has to take the step.

For those of you who are trapped, please know that freedom is only a phone call away. You are strong, resilient, and loved by God. He loves you fully and without reservation and has never left you. Find a safe place to go, a safe person to call, when you are ready.

For those of you working with victims, know that their journey to readiness can take months or even years. I know because it took me years to be ready to move out of victimization. Patience is important. Offer help, love openly, listen to their stories and struggles, and be nonjudgmental.

Much of this process isn't pretty, but when a victim, male or female, is ready to step away, the new life can be amazing. It's a joy to be part of a victim's move into victory.

Love, Leslie

Join the Revolt

1. Look into GED programs in your area. If you need your GED, make the call to start the process. There are programs to help you prepare. If you are working with victimized individuals, create a list of places that will help facilitate the GED process. Also, create a step-by-step guide to getting a GED.

2. Think about times you've heard others (or yourself) talk down to or about victimized individuals, or generalize about the reasons they live the lives they do. How might you have stood up to those wrong assumptions? What could you have said? Write down a few ideas about what you can say the next time you hear people making assumptions about victims of prostitution.

3. Reflect on the events in your life that have affected you deeply. Record in a journal how those events affected you and why you still carry those scars. Be honest and hold nothing back. Who do you need to forgive? Who do you need to ask for forgiveness?

4. Create a list of resources available for those who are victims of prostitution, addictions, homelessness, and alcoholism. This can include homeless shelters, rehab programs, acute detox centers, mental health facilities, food programs, programs such as Sacred Beginnings, and others. Include phone numbers, emails, and websites so you and your team know who to call when specific issues arise. Hand out the list to everyone on your team who works with these individuals.

5. Contact one of the programs on your list and see what their needs are, then work on meeting those needs. Perhaps a nonprofit needs monetary donations or donations of winter coats and boots; perhaps a homeless shelter needs cleaning supplies, sheet sets, or mattresses. Organize a drive to gather supplies and donate them.

Chapter 9

REBIRTH

Sacred Beginnings Women's Transitional Program opened its doors in 2005 and has since served more than thirty-five hundred women. Some stay for a day, others for months, others for years, and some have become peer mentors and victim advocates who work alongside me in street outreach. Some just need kind words over the phone; others need extensive help. Some relapse; others stay clean and go to college, get married, build a career, and mend broken relationships. And some have died.

Sacred Beginnings offers trauma counseling, peer mentoring, group therapy, life-skills coaching, education and career counseling, and optional Bible studies and spiritual discipleship. It is the first survivor-led, peer-mentored program for individuals who have been sexually exploited and trafficked in the state of Michigan. Its cozy rooms, soft quilts, and soothing decor are often a far cry from the lonely rooms and filthy streets many women have experienced for years. All individuals are loved and accepted here.

One young woman called me after her pimp-husband beat her badly and tried to set her on fire. We had been talking on the phone for about week before this event. She wanted to leave, but it took nearly being killed and set on fire for her to make the move.

We sat in one of the Sacred Beginnings houses, and she told me about her life and how she got involved in the streets. She showed me her physical scars. She had emotional scars she needed to talk about too, but I didn't press her. I understand as a trafficking survivor that we tell our stories in our own time. It didn't take long before she opened up.

"Miss Leslie, I'm dying of AIDS. I was scared to tell you because I didn't think you'd accept me into the program. I'll leave if you want me to," she said.

"No, no, no, no. You don't have to leave," I responded. I held her close as she sobbed, allowing her to let go of the pain and the fear of rejection. I let my arms and the quietness of the moment tell her that no matter what, there was no judgment here and she was safe.

"When I leave this earth, I want to be drug-free and with no regrets," she said softly.

We talked about whether she believed in God or some kind of higher power. When she said no, I said, "I understand because I was once that person who didn't believe in God."

I didn't push her on spiritual matters, but I did walk around singing old Negro spirituals whenever I was at the house, as I've always done. I also led a group for prostituted individuals that was open to anyone who was involved in the game, whether in or out; this wounded young woman followed me everywhere, so there she was, sitting next to me as I led that group. She never said a word, but she was clearly listening.

"Miss Leslie," she said on the phone about a month later, "can you come over for a one-on-one session with me? I really need to talk to you."

I went right over.

"Miss Leslie, I listened to you talk about God and how you used to not believe either. I've listened to your story, and I want to know how to connect with God. With all the hate and abuse and pain, all the negative things that have happened, can you and God help me find the positives so that when I leave this earth, I'll know where I'm going? It used to be that I knew I was going to hell and I didn't care because hell couldn't be worse than my hell on earth."

I started praying and singing along with the old Negro spirituals "Lord, Don't Move the Mountain" and "Goin' Up Yonder" that played in the background. We listened to the powerful songs for about thirty minutes, me trying to hold back tears as I prayed and waited. I finally turned to look at her, and her face was so serene, so at peace. She had tears rolling down her cheeks. That moment was so beautiful. I knew God was in the room with us.

This precious child of God knew she had little time left on earth, but now she knew she'd have eternity in heaven. She went with me to church before she started to get real sick from the AIDS ravaging her body and her mind. She was in and out of the hospital, with me and others from Sacred Beginnings at her bedside. She was so at peace knowing we were there, just because we loved her, and would be at her side to the end.

Inevitably, we knew it would be her final trip to the hospital when we called the ambulance seven months later. She knew she wasn't coming back to Sacred Beginnings. I got in touch with her mother, who was caring for her children out of town. She brought this woman's children and her siblings to the hospital to say their final goodbyes.

Heaven—that was my name for her—looked at me and said, "Miss Leslie, I love you."

"I love you too," I replied, barely able to speak.

"I know I'm going up yonder," she said with a big smile on her ravaged face.

I looked at her with tears in my eyes and said, "Oh yes you are, baby. Yes, you are going up yonder."

I went into the bathroom and cried, then came and sat with her family. Later that night, her mom called and said she passed peacefully in her sleep; her daughter was finally at peace and had no more pain. I was devastated but grateful at the same time that I had been privileged to meet such a beautiful soul and assist her in leaving this world with no regrets.

I learned through this experience that my true kingdom mission is to play my part in assisting victims to freedom, helping them learn a new way of life far from pain and trauma, helping them believe that hope is real and powerful and that freedom is possible.

Toward the end of her life, even as she faced death, Heaven kept a smile on her face. She got treatment for AIDS, but with the prostitution and drug abuse, she lacked the early-intervention care she needed. By the time she was diagnosed, it was too late for her.

I knew Heaven for almost a year; I called her Heaven because she was heaven on earth, and that's where she is now. Heaven was in her twenties and had gotten AIDS from a trick. She died drug-free and free from her past. Her future is entirely glorious.

Stories of Love

There are so many stories like Heaven's. When you show love to people, it gives them a chance to learn and grow.

Another young lady called, and I went to pick her up. She stood on the street corner with her bags, pouring rain drenching her heart and her belongings. She, too, had AIDS. The doctor had told her she had six months to live, but she had used up three of those months getting high so had only three months left.

"That devil is a d--- liar. We ain't even going to speak of it," I told her. "The God I know produces miracles every day; I'm one of his living miracles."

That was nearly ten years ago. She is still alive today and living free, the AIDS undetectable. She got back into treatment, but

I credit her healing to God. I prayed and prayed over that girl, and she prayed just as often.

One young lady came to me unable to read or write. She was in her early twenties, and I didn't know if she'd ever been to school. Next thing you know, here came her mother to Sacred Beginnings. Both of them were in our program, but all her mother did was berate and belittle this girl and make false promises, including that she'd quit using drugs. The mother never did quit. The daughter kept using too, relapsing because the bond she wanted and needed with her mother was nonexistent. But there was something about her, so I kept taking her back into the program. She had a sweet innocence; she was such a cute, funny little thing.

I bought the whole set of Dr. Seuss books—*The Cat in the Hat, Green Eggs and Ham, Hop on Pop,* and the rest—and I sat down every day and read to her. It took me back to my childhood because I loved those books. Loving those books made it easier to read them to her. It was beautiful because she was so interested and those books kept her attention as we sounded out the letters and syllables together. Eventually I found out about the Literacy Center of West Michigan. They taught her to read during the day, and I had her at night at Sacred Beginnings. She got clean and moved out, and she stayed clean and continued her education.

That beautiful girl recently graduated with a bachelor's degree in criminal justice from Grand Valley State University (GVSU). She got married and is working, and she's a wonderful mother to her children. Her mother is still in active addiction, but this strong young woman refuses to allow her mother to pull her down. She won't give her mom that power.

One night I received a call from "P," who wanted out of the situation she was in. She came into Sacred Beginnings and stayed eleven months. We kept in contact after she left and began her new life. One day I was sitting in class at GVSU and got a message on my phone from P. She sent me a picture of this tiny little bitty dog—a Pomeranian. She was raising dogs out in the country west of Grand Rapids after leaving Sacred Beginnings. She texted with the picture, "Mama Leslie, this is for you." I don't even like dogs! I told her this, but I kept looking at the picture. There was something about that little dog.

I went out and saw the puppy, who barked like crazy despite being such a tiny thing. She was feisty and I liked her. I still have Gaisha today. Little did I know Gaisha would become my therapy dog and trusted companion for years. When I had to rehome my big dog, Raja, I called P. She came the next day to get Raja, who I know will have a loving and kind home thanks to one woman who had the courage to get out of the life.

It breaks my heart to know there are people out there who don't know what love looks like. It's so twisted for people out on the streets. I've seen mothers sell their children to the dope man for a hit. I've seen mothers turn their children out to a life of prostitution. I've seen young girls so abused that they couldn't stand being confined in any space and ran away every time. I've seen a girl so abused by her own family that she thought having sex with someone who wasn't a blood relative was wrong. There are no boundaries in the life: white, black, brown, men, women, children, adults, transgender people.

All are victims of exploitation.

Every Life Worth Saving

Each individual in every situation is worth going that extra mile for. I do street outreach on weekends, walking or driving in the night to talk to women on the streets of Grand Rapids and other cities. I offer them a Blessed Bag, pray with them if they want me to, give them a hug and a smile, and just meet them right where they are. I let them know they are loved and somebody special regardless of what they think of themselves and what anybody says about them.

People don't know that just a smile can brighten someone's day. Out there on the streets, no one smiles or says hello. It's always something negative—a look, a comment, name-calling, people throwing pennies at them as they stand on the corner. This negativity doesn't come from just the johns and pimps; it's also from the people who drive by and see them on the street. I know all about those horrible things because they've happened to me, and I want to offer something positive to the people I see on the streets.

So I hand out Blessed Bags. Each Blessed Bag, put together by volunteers, includes a regular-sized lotion, soap, shampoo and conditioner, socks, a toothbrush and toothpaste, food items, a water bottle, a note, and a resource card with local programs. Some volunteers add cologne, nail polish, and lipstick. Every Blessed Bag includes my business card.

I might hand out five Blessed Bags one night, ten the next. I might do ministry in two cities in one night, driving from one to the other for a few hours of talking to prostituted individuals. Sometimes I get a hotel room and try to reach these individuals in Detroit one night and nearby Jackson the next.

One recent winter night, I was doing outreach when I pulled into a parking lot and saw a lady holding a hamburger over a cardboard box with steam coming up out of it. She had positioned the box over a sewer grate to trap the warm air rising to street level; she was trying to warm both the hamburger and her freezing feet. I gave her my business card and a Blessed Bag. I couldn't do anything at that time except hug her, and as I walked away, tears poured down my cheeks.

Not too many months later, I received a call.

"You might not remember me, but I'm the lady who was by the sewer with the box. You gave me your card," she said. "I wanted to tell you that I'm in a recovery house and to thank you for even stopping to talk to me. Leslie, I'm not getting raped or beat up anymore."

I sat on my couch and cried. "I'm so proud of you," I said.

"I'm doing good. I kept that card all these months."

"If you ever want to talk, you give me a call," I said, tears still falling. "If you need me, call."

These kinds of calls give so much meaning to what I do. I am told so many traumatic stories, but little do they know that I've lived many of those stories. We can talk for weeks or months as we build trust. Some come in and begin working on their issues, but it gets overwhelming and they go right back to the life. I see the causes; I see the effects. I see the ruin and the relapses. I see the joy and the pain, the life and the death, the rebirth and the new life.

They all call eventually.

Creating a Haven

I get a lot of women who come to Sacred Beginnings from prison. They have heard about me through word of mouth, perhaps at the prison, and write me, needing a place to go when they get released. I also get calls from social workers, lawyers, doctors, police, and women who got my business card in a Blessed Bag, who I met on the streets, or who heard about me from a friend.

I interview each woman over the phone or in person before they come to Sacred Beginnings. Each one is drug tested before they come on the premises—I've had women fail the drug test and not be able to come—then we sit down and talk with the other women in the program. These women who will live with the new person can ask questions of her if they want to, which helps ease their stress about who is coming into the house. It helps empower them as they get to see the process and have some say in the matter.

One thing I've learned is that each of us is going to meet the same people again and again. An individual may know another person from the streets and have had bad interactions with them, but part of healing is learning to let bygones be bygones.

Once these interviews are completed and all are willing, the new resident is invited to come into Sacred Beginnings. Drug screening is done periodically to make sure the women are complying with the rules. Sometimes a woman doesn't comply and is asked to leave. She may get a second chance, but not always. It all depends on her prior activity and willingness to engage in the program.

One resident was at Sacred Beginnings about six months before I heard her full story. She was from Grand Rapids, but at the time she was in a small town north of the city. She was seeking help, but the staff at the local facility said that there was a lot of racial stuff going on and that perhaps she, as a black woman, wasn't a good fit for their program.

She headed back to Grand Rapids, at a loss about what to do next. She heard of Leslie King and Sacred Beginnings but was hesitant to make that first call. She finally did.

"You were in Ludington, right?" I said over the phone. "People have been asking me to look for you."

"That was a crazy day," she later recalled. "I prayed and God answered. Miss Leslie knew about me way before I made that call."

During our first call, I told her there were several things she needed to do before coming to Sacred Beginnings, including entering into a drug treatment program. She did everything she needed to do, and when she came out the door of the rehab facility, I was there waiting for her.

"Miss Leslie hugged me and took me home," she said later, with tears in her eyes. "I didn't want to die out there, but I didn't know what else to do."

Sacred Beginnings is a sacred place for survivors. "It's like a transfer station out of darkness into light," she said. "Miss Leslie enabled and strengthened the little bit of hope I had at that time. I wished my life could change and hoped it could, but now I believe that my life really can change. Ain't no way anyone can help me if they haven't been through it, but Miss Leslie has. She makes you feel loved and that you have worth."

Not Everyone Makes It Out of the Game

A lot of women come through the program and do well, but then they leave and get into relationships without having worked enough on themselves. The next time I do outreach, there they are on the street again. But I don't judge them because I remember when it was me back out there on the streets after going through a program.

Several times I've done outreach and stood there talking with a woman, and next thing I know I find out she's dead. I pick up a newspaper and it says, "Prostitute Found Dead," which is the media labeling her like she's nothing. So many are killed by tricks, first raped and then thrown out of their vehicle to die alone on the side of the road.

I remember years ago a young boy was selling himself for a place to stay. I call it survival sex. He got thrown out of a truck, was severely beaten, and had his mouth and eyes superglued shut. Everything bad that can happen to a person has happened to those who live on the streets. The sad thing is, almost nobody's going to believe them and almost nobody cares.

I took it especially hard when one woman I had just talked to was set on fire. A lot of things ran through my head. Was she dead before she was set on fire? I struggled with myself, wondering if I'd only done this or that, could she have been saved? I used to take it really personally and second-guess myself when one of the women ended up dead. Now, it still hurts me down deep, but I know I did all I could and will always have good memories of them and pray for their families. Then I go back out on the streets and do outreach even harder, doing my best to help each one see and come into the light.

While there are a lot of good outcomes to the work of Sacred Beginnings, there are a lot of unhappy endings too. Women can't stay clean; they are addicted to life on the streets and go back out there; they have a hard time adjusting to rules. Sometimes there are tragedies no one could have predicted.

One young lady, probably in her twenties, was staying at Sacred Beginnings and doing very well, in my estimation. She was going to her meetings and abiding by the rules. This girl had a magnetic smile; she was beautiful in so many ways.

For some reason, though, she experienced a lot of pain in her abdomen. I'd find her doubled up in pain sometimes. She kept going to a local hospital here in Grand Rapids and telling them she was sick and in pain, but they didn't treat her, instead assuming she was a drug seeker. Three or four times she visited the hospital, but nothing was done for her.

Finally, one time they did keep her, but she was angry at the way they were treating her. I talked to her on the phone, listening as she described how they spoke to her. It wasn't good and made me angry too.

She called a longtime-sober friend from Narcotics Anonymous to come get her; he took her directly from the hospital to Sacred Beginnings. She spent time talking to and laughing with the women living there that evening, sharing her beautiful smile with all of them. I talked to her as well, and she said she was OK. I thought so too.

She went to her room and went to sleep. Come morning, however, she was dead.

Her roommate said that during the night she heard her gargling, which I'm convinced was the death rattle.

Her mother called me that morning, wondering where her

daughter was; she knew she had left the hospital but hadn't been able to get ahold of her. In the meantime, I was driving over to the house because the women had called and were hysterical, stating that one of the women was dead.

When I got there, the coroner was putting her body into the bag for removal. "Wait a minute," I said, and leaned over and gave her a kiss on the forehead.

Her mother called me again.

"She went to sleep and didn't wake up," I told her. "She's dead."

She screamed and screamed. She talked about how she usually went with her daughter to the hospital to advocate for her because of the way they treated her, but this time her daughter hadn't wanted her there.

Finally she said this as we both cried: "Leslie, thank you for not allowing my daughter to die in an alley or somewhere all alone."

I didn't even know how to respond.

Her mother brought pictures of this girl to the recovery house. Those pictures are still there, like a guardian angel for the house. Later I and my outreach team, along with several women from Sacred Beginnings, went to South Division, home of the Stroll, and held a candlelight vigil for this young woman who died too soon. We tied purple ribbons around our arms in her honor.

As we held the vigil, a police officer pulled up. He got out of the car to talk to us, then tied a purple ribbon to his cruiser. I was so awed by that.

To this day, the girl's mother and I are still close.

Educating the Public

My mission is to protect and to love those who are still lost in the darkness. But part of doing that is educating everyone else about trafficking. I educate them through speaking engagements, outreach, and this book. I talk to prosecutors, judges, police, doctors, nurses, dentists, social workers, and anyone who has some sort of contact with people who may be trafficked. A lot of the time, people don't even know they've been in contact with a victim, so I educate them on the warning signs and what to look for. (You can find out more about warning signs on my website, www.sbtp.org.)

There are also a lot of people out there who think they're doing good but aren't. There is a lot of what I call white-collar pimping going on. White-collar pimping can include entities that are profiting from survivors' trauma and pain by using their stories and likenesses without adequate compensation. Many of these individuals have not been out of the game long enough and have not healed, and are being re-exploited. The abused women think others are trying to help them, not aware that they're being taken advantage of once again. That's the sad part—they're still being used. To me, that's white-collar pimping all day, and it happens more often than people think.

Being used keeps you on guard, just like I had to be when I was on the streets. I meet some of the same kinds of people today that I knew then; they just wear suits and sit behind desks instead of walking the streets like I did. Everyone needs to check their motives, because everyone *has* motives, good or bad or unhealthy. Really studying your motives reveals the true heart behind why you're helping. If your motive is to exploit a person for your personal gain—for pride, control, money, or something else—you know your motive is wrong.

A SACRED BEGINNINGS GRADUATE'S STORY

I met Miss Leslie when she came to Turning Point to talk to us residents. It was my first time in rehab and I didn't know what to do, but something drew me to Miss Leslie. I was so nervous to walk up to her that I waited until she was done talking to everyone else before I finally asked her if she had any rooms left at Sacred Beginnings and could I come.

She came to visit me a couple of times as we got to know each other. Then, on my release date, she picked me up and brought me to her house on Elliott Street. She enrolled me at the Beckwith Adult Education Center and encouraged me to write out my life story, but I didn't know how to read or spell. Every day I said I was going to Beckwith, but instead I just roamed around. I was twenty-three years old and didn't know what the heck I was doing.

The day Leslie said she needed my life story written, I was up all night because I was so nervous. I relapsed and was gone for a couple of days. People kept telling me, "You know Leslie King is looking for you?"

I came back after a week and told her I couldn't meet her expectations. I thought she'd throw me out, but she didn't. She told me to get myself cleaned up and go to sleep. I woke up to find that she had bought a bunch of Dr. Seuss books. She began to help me with reading. I would read the words I recognized, and she'd read the rest. That's when I started to trust her.

Never had nobody sat down and read with me and not got mad at me when I didn't know a word.

I stayed with Leslie on Elliott Street for six months, then had a really bad relapse. I was so ashamed and didn't want to tell her, so I moved out. I moved in with someone else, but then went missing for a few days. Eventually I moved back in with my mom, who was in her addiction. I went missing again. This time I was found in or beside (I never found out which) the dumpster outside Freyling's Restaurant. When I came to, the officers said my mom and stepdad were looking for me. They had gone through my purse while I was out and found my relapse prevention plan.

They called my support people, and they called Leslie.

I thought my support person was driving me to jail or to rehab, but instead we pulled up to Leslie's house. The women there took me to Walmart and bought me toiletries and a few outfits. I didn't know what was going on or what would happen next, but when we got back in the car, Miss Leslie said, "I care about you and love you and don't want to see you out there. We're going to try this again. I think there is something for you to do in this world."

I checked back into Turning Point, had a mental breakdown and went to Forest View, a psychiatric facility, returned to Turning Point, and then spent 121 days at a women's residential home. Leslie brought me clothes and came to visit, and when I was finished, she picked me up and took me to a Sacred Beginnings house on Fisk Road, where I stayed for a year.

I qualified for a Section 8 Housing Choice Voucher, so I found an apartment with Leslie's help, got my son back (he's eighteen now), and ended up getting married. I got custody of my little sister when she was thirteen, and I now have two sons.

I probably wouldn't be here if it wasn't for Miss Leslie. She has pulled me out of houses before, has come looking for me, and hovered and mothered me. I never had anybody love on me like Leslie did. On March 7, 2008, I got clean. I did it without antidepressants or anything to take away the shakes. It was me having to deal with me.

I have an associate's degree in juvenile services and substance abuse counseling from Grand Rapids Community College and a bachelor's degree in criminal justice from Ferris State University. I now work at Arbor Circle as a recovery coach and case manager.

I wouldn't be able to relate to the population I work with if I hadn't gone through all these experiences. One thing I tell the girls I work with is that they have to find their "Now what?" They can't stay in the same place. Asking themselves "Now what?" is the first baby step to moving forward. I also tell people in addiction that if they have a feeling that something is wrong, they should follow that instinct and seek help from someone they trust. Not sharing and keeping it all in is worse for you than letting someone in to help you.

I don't know where I would be without Leslie. She's my mom and I love her. I appreciate her so much for taking me under her wing and showing me there is a better way of living life.

Living this life sober is so much better than what I had before.

Dear Reader,

The road to freedom isn't easy. It takes hard work, patience, understanding, learning forgiveness, and help. But you can do it—just not alone. Find those who can help you, such as through a program like Sacred Beginnings. You may find a program in your city or state, but don't be afraid to relocate if you have to. Remember, freedom starts with taking that first step.

For those of you not on the streets, you never know what a kind word, a smile, a bag of supplies, or a single business card can do. Keep doing what you are called to do, time after time after time. You can't know how God will use your faithfulness to save a life.

God wants to use each of us to accomplish his purposes. He wants to use you to help victims of trafficking. I encourage you to look hard at your motives for helping; are your motives about you or about helping those who need help the most?

For those of you in the life, God wants to save you from bondage and bring you into a new life of freedom. I implore you to let him.

Love, Leslie

Join the Revolt

1. Create a list of the local organizations in your city or area where victims of trafficking and abuse can find safety. Visit each one if you can so you know what sort of place you are recommending to victims.

2. Volunteer at a hotline for victims of sexual exploitation. Learn firsthand the protocols for talking with these individuals and the resources available. Learn as much as you can from the training you receive.

3. Ask local organizations such as Sacred Beginnings what sort of donations they can use. Be very specific in your giving by truly listening to what these programs need.

4. Look carefully at your motives for wanting to help trafficked individuals. Are you helping from a heart of caring and love, or are you more interesting in looking good at church or in front of your friends? Dig deep into your own heart. Ask Jesus to help.

5. Think carefully about how you, your nonprofit, or your ministry are using the stories of victims of exploitation. Are you using their stories with permission to help raise funds or to put together your own program or speaking engagements? Are you offering compensation for using their stories? How might you or your ministry need to rethink this issue?

Chapter 10

LIFE LESSONS

My first child was born when I was fifteen and my second son when I was in my twenties. My third and fourth sons were born in the early 1990s when I was deep into life on the streets. My mom adopted and raised my first two boys, which I thank God for every day. Even though we lived in the same community, I rarely saw them, and when I did, it was usually from a distance. My other two sons were adopted by the same woman, one as a newborn and the other at three years old. My mom regrets she wasn't able to adopt them too, but she was battling breast cancer during that time.

My fifth son isn't my child by birth, but he is a child of my heart. I married three years after I got clean and sober, choosing a man in recovery, just as I was. He had a young son he had no contact with, whose mother ended up dying when he was a young child.

"You need to go get your son," I told my husband. I assisted him in getting custody of his boy, but my husband kept relapsing into his old way of life. He used that child as a pawn in our relationship; he knew how much I loved that little boy, so I wouldn't leave him despite his dope-fiend behavior. I eventually divorced him, but the child stayed with me, and I loved and raised him as my own. It felt like God gave me another chance at motherhood with that boy. I was finally a mother with a son to raise on my own.

Years later, I received a call and the person asked if I was Leslie. "Yes, this is Leslie," I said.

The man on the phone told me he was my youngest son. I started crying immediately. Then I asked him about his brother, my other son. When my boy told me his brother had been murdered right here on the streets of Grand Rapids in 2012, I lost it. I was unhinged and lost all faith in God at that point too.

I searched Google for his name and put in "murdered in Grand Rapids," and the story popped up. Turns out he had been murdered on the same street where I was doing outreach. I wondered if my son had seen me and not said anything. I feel like he had been looking for me. I wondered, too, if I had seen him and not known it. I asked myself, How many times had I looked into his face and passed him by? How many times had he tried to speak with me but been too afraid? Little did I know he was buried just a few blocks from where I lived.

When I heard about my son's death, I was numb and angry. Here I went again asking God why. "Why did you take my son? I got my life together and did everything you asked of me, and you took my son." I was twelve years sober at that point. I locked myself in my room for three days. I lay in a fetal position, crying and mourning, feeling so much shame and guilt, feeling suicidal, saying, "If I had done this or that, this wouldn't have happened." I blamed myself for my son's death. If I had seen him, I could have helped him. My heart was broken.

On the third day, I was lying in bed and heard chains. They were very faint. Then the chains became louder and louder and louder, and then *boom!* I jumped out of bed, ran downstairs, opened up all the curtains, and asked my children for my keys. They had taken them away, because they were worried I would relapse. But I went straight out my door and went back to outreach, because I didn't want another woman—another mother—to experience the pain that I was going through.

Days later I found his grave and collapsed on it, sobbing, digging my fingers into his gravesite, trying to get at my son. But something happened as I got up from that dirt. Just as I stood up, just as I had gotten up from three days of mourning, and just as I stood before God in my sin, I rose clean. I was forgiven. I was a new person. I rose even more dedicated than ever to helping women find freedom from a life of prostitution and substance abuse, and to praying that my pain and suffering wouldn't become theirs.

I never wanted my children to think that I abandoned them or gave them up because I didn't want them or didn't love them. At that time, the best love I could show my children was to give them to someone who could love and care for them. I refused to drag my children through hell with me. I was spiritually, emotionally, and mentally void at that time.

I now have a wonderful relationship with my boys. As my granddaughters say, "You're the coolest granny ever." I know the relationship with my children has been redeemed. My family is everything to me. I love them. I love cooking for them, I love being their mom, and I love my relationship with every one of them.

My mom and I are in a wonderful place too. I talk to her every day, though I don't see her because she now lives in Mesa, Arizona. She moved there to get away from the cold, which is terrible for her arthritis, and my sister lives not far from her.

As I often say, "My mom prayed me through those years when I was too stupid to pray for myself."

Here's what my mom has to say about her life then and now.

LESLIE'S MOTHER'S STORY

For twenty years, every night I prayed that no one would call me and tell me they had found Leslie's body. It was hell for me all those years, but God in his timing granted my wish.

It was an honor when Bethany Christian Services called me and asked if I wanted to adopt Leslie's older boys. I didn't hesitate; I said yes right away. I was able to give them love and show them the love I wasn't able to show to my own children when I was younger. I also allowed them to be around their mother when she was in a good place to let them know that Leslie was their birth mother.

I remember a time when I visited Leslie in jail. I had been going through chemo for breast cancer and had lost almost all my hair. She asked me why I was wearing a scarf, so I pulled it off. She was pretty horrified to see me with maybe one piece of hair on my head.

I told her, "I didn't put quitters on this earth." This applied to both me and her. "No quitters on this earth," I said again.

There is nothing but the grace of God. You'll go through trials and tribulations, but the grace of God will get you through. By the grace of God, my children know how to pick up the phone and talk to me. I had to always be the strong one so my children could be strong.

When I think of all my kids, I say, "Thank you, Jesus. You turned the light on, and now I can say, 'I love you.'"

When I look at Leslie, I am so proud of her accomplishments, but I'm more proud that God brought her through all of that. I'm proud to say that God granted my wish and turned my child around, and now she's helping other women.

I work two days a week as a home health aide these days. I can't sit at home waiting for death to come for me. I go to two different people's homes and help them four hours a day. This is something I never thought I'd be doing, but I'm really enjoying it. I laugh with them, share stories, listen to their stories. It's so fulfilling. Also, I walk two miles every day. At first I had a small apartment, then a bigger one, and people kept giving me stuff for the apartment. God made a way for me here.

I have this message for women who are stuck in some way in their lives, whether in addiction or sex trafficking, or who are having a rough time for one reason or another. My message is to never give up. When I was a kid and was frustrated about something, I'd grab the Bible, close my eyes, flip open the Bible, and put my finger on a spot. I'd read that passage until it said something to me. This taught me to never give up, to never ignore God.

I say that to women too. Never give up. Never let your spiritual side die. Regardless of what people are saying in the world or are telling you, God is still standing. My proof is me and my children. So hold on. The devil is here to steal, kill, and destroy, but you are a beautiful person made in God's image. He never said life would be easy, but it will all be worth it in the end.

◊ ◊ ◊

I remember surprising my mom for her birthday several years ago. I flew to Arizona to see her. When my mom got to my sister's friend's house and walked in the door, she was surprised to smell food; my sister can't boil an egg.

Mama was so surprised when I walked into the room. Her reaction scared me so bad that I thought she was going to have a heart attack. She was so excited to see me, as I was her. Like I've said before, she's the wind beneath my wings.

When I first started doing speaking engagements, I was afraid to say certain things because I didn't want to hurt her. But I said them anyway, knowing I had to tell the truth. Yet every time I came off that stage after telling the truth, my mom was the first person to hug me.

THE STORY OF JOHAN KING (LESLIE'S OLDEST SON)

I remember walking home from school with my little brother, and we'd get to the end of our street and smell food in the air. We'd have an inclination, then get home and my mom would be there. She'd embrace us and be happy to see us. She'd be there two or three days, and it was good, but then she'd be gone. Two years later, she might show up again.

In 1994, she got herself clean to get back my two younger brothers. It was good to see her trying to get better, and it surprised me how well she was doing. Then she vanished again, and my little brothers were raised elsewhere. Our family grew up apart, all of us separated a lot. But now when I see my mom, we feel the love in the room. I have a relationship with one of my younger brothers, who I found on Facebook. We are two peas in a pod, and I thank my mom for that.

She always wanted the best for us—I honestly believe that. My mom didn't take us through her lifestyle, which is why my grandma raised us. Being with Grandma was the best place for me and made me the man I am. She and my mom are responsible for where I am today.

What my mom is doing right now is nothing short of amazing. I can't change the past, but I can change going forward. We've got the best relationship we've ever had. I told her that she may have missed motherhood, but she can pay it forward by being a grandma. She loves that role, and she's an awesome grandma. My mom is my heart.

◊ ◊ ◊

Cause and Effect

My years as a victim of prostitution and substance abuse have affected my life. I didn't get through those years unscathed.

In my forties, I noticed I'd drive someplace and forget where I was going, or I'd forget in the middle of a sentence what I meant to say. At first I thought I had dementia, but it wasn't dementia. I and several other survivors had been discussing traumatic brain injury (TBI) and researching symptoms and injuries associated with TBI. I had had multiple concussions from being hit by tricks, thrown out of cars, and beaten by my pimp. We are now pretty sure TBI is one of the illnesses many victims of prostitution suffer from due to the violence that comes with being in the life.

I was also diagnosed with PTSD, manic depression caused by all the trauma, and anxiety. Those are from living my life in fear, constantly on a hair trigger, and not knowing what was coming next. I am still triggered by certain smells or memories. In my fifties, I was diagnosed with ADHD (I've probably had it since childhood), night terrors, and Prinzmetal's angina, which is a heart condition caused by cocaine abuse. I've had both hips replaced, probably a result of years of walking, walking, walking the streets of numerous Strolls in many cities in various states.

THE STORY OF A VICTIM'S DAUGHTER

I was asked to write a letter in my English class during my first week of college to the most influential person I knew. The other students had no problem with this topic and started writing away like it was the easiest thing they had ever done. This wasn't the case for me. You see, when you grow up with parents in active addiction, you have nobody to look up to—you are alone. The feelings I remember so well as a child are the same feelings that still impact me today: guilt, denial, anxiety, helplessness, anger, and depression. Being the child of an addict is like being addicted to a drug I never got the chance to use while still enduring the same side effects.

My father is a raging alcoholic, and my mother's drug of choice was cocaine. Imagine everyone knowing why your mom acts the way she does and why she weighs so little all of a sudden. Some people ask and try to get details, and some just look at you like you are a rescue puppy that nobody wants. If I had to use one word to describe the memories of my childhood, it would be *pain*. Not the type of pain when you get a paper cut and it heals over after a week. No, the agony from the traumas of my childhood has been embedded so deep that it will follow me for my lifetime.

I lived with my father during my early teenage years and reached the lowest point in my life when my mother was in active addiction. I tried to take away the pain by trying to take my own life. I attempted suicide . . . twice. In that moment, time stops and all you can do is feel—no thinking or rationalizing, just feeling. You're engulfed by the darkness and so tired of fighting to get to the surface, so you just sit there and accept it. I was fifteen.

My best friend at that time saved my life. He found me nearly lifeless on my bedroom floor from the countless pills I swallowed in an effort to escape. I was rushed to the hospital in an ambulance, both times. I vaguely remember the smell of the paramedic's rubber gloves as he shook my pill bottles in front of my face, asking me how many I took as I flashed in and out of consciousness. As badly as I wanted it to end, my fight wasn't over. I made a full recovery both times.

The self-hate that evolved from my mother's addiction was more than any child should ever bear. I hated my mother and my father. I hated the world for being cruel, but mostly I hated myself. Trying to convince myself that I was allowed to take up space on this earth was like writing with my left hand when I was born to use my right. This is life for a child of an addict.

Sometimes you must explain the gory before you can get to the glory. So, to answer the question, "Who is the most influential person I know?" my answer is Ms. Leslie King. Leslie saved my mom's life. Because of Leslie, my mom now has three years of sobriety and is helping run one of Leslie's recovery homes with Sacred

Beginnings. I am now rebuilding my relationship with my mother, and it has never been more beautiful.

There was a point in my life when I never thought I would have the chance to go to college, but Leslie has inspired me to chase my dreams and pursue a degree in social work so that one day I can help women the same way she helped my mom. I am now a college freshman, and I am proud to say I currently hold a 3.8 GPA. I don't think that would have ever been possible without Leslie as my inspiration.

Both Leslie and my mother have taught me that anything is achievable with hard work, patience, and dedication. Leslie inspires me to want to make a positive change in the world. It is truly an honor and a blessing to have had the opportunity to meet someone as selfless and openhearted as Leslie. Even though my life has not always been easy, I am thankful for everything I have gone through, and I wouldn't change anything because it has made me into the strong and resilient woman I am today.

◊ ◊ ◊

The Real Start of Slavery

Legal slavery existed in the United States from before the country was founded and meant the enslavement of black people. While slavery is often talked about as this one kind of institutional enslavement, so many of us are still treated the same way. Slavery, pimping and pandering (the practice of procuring a person to be used for prostitution), and human trafficking and sexual exploitation all result in the same thing: people being sold. Whether people are being sold to work a plantation or being sold to service tricks, it's all the same game. Pray for an end to all these games. Pray to end the selling of one person for the benefit of another.

Years of experience as a traumatized and trafficked woman myself, a street outreach worker, a survivor leader, a motivational speaker, and the founder of Sacred Beginnings have shown me a thing or two about assisting victims of trafficking and other traumas. Let me address a number of groups about working with these individuals.

To Health-Care Workers

1. *Be nonjudgmental.* You may see her dirty, beat up, and high. You'll see she's been in your emergency room before and immediately tag her as a user. All these indicators—injuries, drugs, repeated ER visits, female-related symptoms—are red flags of victimization. Don't just treat the outer, visual wounds; connect the dots that this person is a victim and should be treated as such. Remember the girl who died at my house? Her experience makes me ask myself, How many individuals have died because of lack of care, understanding, and empathy? How many individuals have we lost because of inadequate health care, in part because they didn't want to go to a care provider, knowing how they would be treated? We are treated like expendable trash by pimps and johns, but we shouldn't be treated that way by people who should be helping us.

2. *Be empathetic.* Nobody was born this way. Ask yourself what caused her to fall this far. This is someone's daughter, son, niece, sister, mother. She or he is somebody to somebody.

3. *Be diligent.* Who is around the individual when he or she comes in? Is that person trying to control the narrative by not allowing him or her to answer questions? Does he or she avoid eye contact with you? Is he or she hesitant to

answer questions? If you can answer yes to these questions, you could be dealing with a victim.

4. *Stay educated.* Attend trainings and seminars, especially those led by survivors who have been out of the life for quite some time and have really worked on themselves so they can speak into the realities of victimization. Staying educated is important because there is no single age, gender, or color associated with those who are trafficked. A lot of times you may think someone is in a domestic violence situation, but it's really trafficking. All people from all walks of life can fall prey to victimization.

Every hospital should have a survivor working in the ER or on call. That survivor will be able to extract information most healthcare providers can't and will see the cues that are so easily missed. Wound knows wound, so the patient won't be afraid to speak to a survivor. If there is a pimp or a bottom in the room, the survivor will recognize that instantly.

The survivor on staff can be a liaison between the patient and the medical staff. Doctors are paid a lot of money to treat people, but they often come in with no feeling or emotion. Nurses are overworked, tired, and exasperated. I wouldn't talk to any of them either. Call a lived-experience expert who can help in ways beyond medical professionals. When your ER liaison is unavailable, have a plan B in place.

Pursue having someone come in to your hospital or office to provide training. Also, don't think that just because you work in the suburbs or a rural area that victims aren't going to come in. Victimization is everywhere, and you need to be prepared.

To Law Enforcement and First Responders

1. *Be nonjudgmental.* You don't know his or her story. When police officers come across individuals who are mean and sarcastic, they tend to believe the individual deserved what they got, without knowing their stories. When I worked with SWAPP, I spoke to officers about what these victims had gone through, their childhoods, and their many traumas. There was not a dry eye in the room afterward. They hadn't known. Learn the victims' stories.

2. *Be respectful.* When you have to arrest victims of prostitution, treat these women and men with respect. Treat them like you would anyone else. Don't call them names and treat them like dirt. Each one is a human just like you.

3. *Arrest the johns.* I was in a class at Grand Rapids Community College, speaking alongside police officers. The students asked why the johns weren't arrested and their names put in the paper. The officers said it was a liability issue. The johns might sue. *What?* I immediately got angry. Nobody is scared about liability when they label an individual victim as a prostitute and put their picture, name, and record in the media. Please, do your jobs without fear, and perhaps this cycle can end. I was asked once what a john looked like, and I laughed. I said the majority of johns are middle-aged white men, some older white men and some younger. They could be your father, husband, uncle, neighbor, pastor, local police officer, elected official—anyone. The men who nearly killed me didn't look any different from the many other johns I saw.

4. *Offer help.* Jail is more than just jail. An individual isn't going to leave the life until they are ready, but if you keep locking them up, that's still victimization. On the other

hand, they could wind up dead out on the streets. I'm convinced that the last time I was locked up saved my life. Jail kept me from being victimized in a different way. This difference speaks to how we objectify victims in jail, how jails don't offer the services they state they offer, and the help victims could receive. Offer help, knowing that it may be turned down. Do it anyway and do it repeatedly. The reality of jail, which I didn't see at the time I was locked up, is that they are places that could offer needed services for individuals who are caught in the life. You never know who is going to come through that locked door. It could be one of your family members.

To the Community at Large

1. *Be vigilant.* Be aware of what's going on in your community. If you think something is wrong or something iffy is going on, nine times out of ten it is. You never know about people, so watch and be aware.

2. *Know that nobody is immune.* I don't care where you live, the things you have, or the things you don't have—people still fall prey to victimization and predators. And predators are everywhere. Know that when a predator gets into someone's mind, the body will follow.

3. *Get involved.* Ask social service agencies, local nonprofits, your school, and/or your church what you can do to help victims of trafficking. You'll be surprised at what you learn and at the ways you can help.

Do You Think You're Ready to Help?

1. *Check your motives.* Make sure you really want to help victims of prostitution and aren't just being nosy. Study your heart before starting this work, and make sure your motives are pure. The work is hard, heartbreaking, and exhausting. It takes a strong, empathetic, nonjudgmental person to work with these victims.

2. *Don't dig.* Don't start by asking them about their lives. Don't start digging and have them open up about something you don't understand. Don't open a wound you don't know how to close. These individuals have severe trust issues. If you violate that trust in any form or fashion, it could send the person back out onto the streets and maybe to their death.

3. *Be open-minded.* Don't be judgmental, critical, or negative. Listen and learn.

4. *Work with professionals.* Work with an agency that has a proven track record of assisting victims. Ask the coordinator what you can do to help, then follow the program instructions for interacting with victims. Don't think that you, with little experience and knowledge in this area, know best. You can do irreparable damage out of ignorance and stubbornness (see point 5).

5. *Don't come Bible thumping.* So many victims have been dragged through the darkness, and many don't believe in God. Spouting Bible verses and laying hands on them isn't going to work. One woman told me that God told her to lay hands on women and pray. I said to her, "Do you know how many people have put their hands on her? Thousands and thousands of hands have been on her in ways you'll never understand. Putting your hands on her without her

permission could end up badly." Also, many people have been abused in the church. I know a woman whose parents were pastors and sold her to people in the church. That's called familial trafficking. Be aware of these kinds of stories. Spiritual authority can easily become a weapon in the wrong hands.

6. *Learn to really listen.* Hear what the person is saying, don't be afraid to ask questions about what you do not understand, and don't be easily offended. You're there to learn.

7. *Watch your words.* A few things to never say: Why didn't you just leave? Why are you doing this? Why don't you make better choices? Why don't you just stop?

CONCLUSION

Now you know my story. Part of it, anyway. There are events and people I will never talk about in this lifetime. There are things I've done that no one will ever know. But God knows, and he loves me without judgment or condition. In fact, he sent his angels to fight for me and others more times than I can count.

As I look back on my life—two very different lives lived in one lifetime—I can honestly say I wouldn't change anything. God uses my past, my victimization, my story to change lives. I am honored that he would use me in his great plan to carry his light to lead a revolt against the darkness.

I am thrilled to be part of a family again. My mother continues to be the wind beneath my wings, my inspiration, my role model. I love my siblings, my sons, and their families. I'm pretty sure I'm the best granny ever. I love that God has turned my pain into my passion.

This book has been a winding journey for me as I relived my childhood, reprocessed trauma, and stepped back into some of the most awful events of my life. It has been a healing journey as well, an opportunity for me to see God's grand scheme for my life through the good, the bad, and the ugly. I've delighted in seeing how God has used my past to create a future that can help bring others out of bondage and into freedom.

My journey, however, isn't over. The work continues. I am out on the streets several nights a week, right alongside God's angels, talking to those still held in bondage, offering them Blessed Bags, and praying with them if they agree. Sacred Beginnings continues its work of bringing light into very dark places, of bringing God's children back from death to life. Thank you, Jesus.

I have so many things I want to do, things I know God wants me to do, and people I pray God wants me to help find light in the darkness. Every life is worth saving, and every person has a kingdom mission on this earth.

I'm already thinking about my next book, where I'll talk about the many traumas and triggers I faced throughout my recovery, how life on the streets and addiction affected my recovery, and how those things can affect someone's recovery. I want to share openly and honestly about the trials and tribulations of becoming a productive citizen. I've talked some about it here, but there is so much more to say to people whose children are in recovery, who are in recovery themselves, and who work with people on the recovery journey.

As the founder and president of Sacred Beginnings and a survivor leader, I speak nationwide on trafficking. I talk to social workers, law enforcement, health-care workers, clergy, and anyone else who may come into contact with trafficked individuals. I want to share with them what I've lived and what I know so they can help others who have so many triggers and so much trauma.

The road to recovery is fraught with twists and turns that are unique to every individual. I pray I can be part of their journeys as I continue on my own journey.

For more information on Sacred Beginnings, visit www.sbtp.org.

ACKNOWLEDGMENTS

My mother, for loving me and praying for me when I could not pray for myself.

My siblings, for always being there for me.

My children, I love you with all that I am. Know that the best love I could give to you at that time in my life was to give you to someone I knew would give you a great life. Not once did I ever stop loving and missing you.

My grandchildren, you bring me so much joy and happiness. You help me to live again.

My husband, you have been such a blessing to me, showing me what true love is.

For all the women who are still trapped in the darkness, know that there is a way out. Just follow the light.

For those who have lost their lives to such evil, you can now rest, as I will not stop fighting until my last breath.

Ann Byle, thank you for assisting me through this book.

SUGGESTED RESOURCES

Futures Against Violence hosts a current and well-vetted list of anti-trafficking resources online at https://www.futures withoutviolence.org/organizational-leadership-training/building -collaborative-responses-to-human-trafficking/. Below, you can find an incomplete list of organizations, nonprofits, and agencies involved in the fight against human trafficking. Many of these organizations have specific resources on topics such as immigration and prostitution, language accessibility, labor trafficking, LGBTQ trafficking victims, children and youth, legal advocacy, and trauma-informed care.

Aequitas, https://aequitasresource.org

Alliance to End Slavery and Trafficking, https://endslavery andtrafficking.org

Asian American Legal Defense and Education Fund, https:// www.aaldef.org

Asista Immigration Assistance, https://asistahelp.org/resource -library/t-visas/

Center for Court Innovation, https://www.courtinnovation.org /areas-of-focus/human-trafficking

Coalition to Abolish Slavery and Trafficking, https://www.castla
.org
Disability Justice, https://disabilityjustice.org
End Abuse of People with Disabilities, https://www.end
abusepwd.org
Freedom Network USA, https://freedomnetworkusa.org
Futures Without Violence, https://www.futureswithoutviolence
.org
Human Trafficking and the State Courts Collaborative, http://
www.htcourts.org
Human Trafficking Legal Center, https://www.htlegalcenter.org
Indian Law Resource Center, https://indianlaw.org
Intercommunity Peace and Justice Center, https://www.ipjc.org
/human-trafficking/
Minnesota Indian Women's Sexual Assault Coalition, https://
www.miwsac.org
My Sisters' Place, https://mspny.org
National Center on Domestic Violence, Trauma, and Mental
Health, http://www.nationalcenterdvtraumamh.org
National Center for Homeless Education, https://nche.ed.gov
National Disability Rights Network, https://www.ndrn.org
National Human Trafficking Hotline, https://humantrafficking
hotline.org, 1-888-373-7888
National Immigrant Women's Advocacy Project, https://www.wcl
.american.edu/impact/initiatives-programs/niwap/
National Indigenous Women's Resource Center, https://www
.niwrc.org
National Resource Center on Justice Involved Women, https://
cjinvolvedwomen.org
National Sexual Violence Resource Center, https://www.nsvrc
.org

National Survivor Network, https://nationalsurvivornetwork
.org

Not for Sale, https://www.notforsalecampaign.org

Office for Victims of Crime, US Department of Justice, https://ovc
.ojp.gov/program/human-trafficking/overview

Office on Trafficking in Persons, US Department of Health and
Human Services, https://www.acf.hhs.gov/otip

Polaris Project, https://polarisproject.org

Runaway and Homeless Youth Training and Technical
Assistance Center, https://www.rhyttac.net

Safe Horizon, https://www.safehorizon.org

Tapestri, https://tapestri.org

The Arc, https://thearc.org

ABOUT THE AUTHOR

Leslie F. King is a survivor of human trafficking and sexual exploitation. She was coerced into the lifestyle of prostitution at the tender age of fifteen and became trapped in the underworld of prostitution and drug addiction for over twenty years. On July 4, 2000, God miraculously saved Leslie and gave her the strength and courage to break free.

Since 2003, Leslie has been intensely engaged in working with individuals who find themselves trapped in the same horrors that she experienced. In 2005, Leslie utilized her experience, expertise, and inspiring example of a renewed life to open Sacred Beginnings, a safe haven that offers hope and healing to trafficking victims. Leslie consults with law enforcement agencies, human service professionals, clergy, and others requesting direction and understanding in working with prostituted individuals. Leslie also speaks at various conferences and academic institutions on the issue of human trafficking.

Leslie is well-respected in her home state of Michigan, where she is often seen boldly conducting street outreach to sexually exploited people during unconventional hours.

Awards and recognitions include:

- 2005 Grand Rapids, MI, Woman of the Year nominee
- 2008 YWCA Advocate of the Year
- 2011 Rising Hero Award
- 2014 "50 Most Influential Women in West Michigan"
- 2018 Michigan Liberator Award
- 2019 Grand Rapids Negro Business and Professional Women's Club Certificate of Achievement
- 2021 African American Leadership Award
- 2021 BBB Trust Award

S A C R E D B E G I N N I N G S

Founded by Leslie in 2005, Sacred Beginnings is the first survivor-led peer mentored program in Michigan for those who have been trafficked. Their mission is to lead the revolution against human trafficking and sexual exploitation by supporting victims on the streets, in the courtroom, and beyond.

Learn more about Sacred Beginnings at www.sbtp.org.